Paul Gascoigne's sensational goal from a free-kick against Arsenal in last season's FA Cup Semi-Final had millions of TV fans off their seats.

D0528601

GAZZA-

Born in Gateshead in May 1967, Paul made his debut for Newcastle United during the 1984-85 season.

He scored 21 goals in 92 League games for Newcastle before moving to Tottenham Hotspur for £2 million in July 1988.

After several appearances as substitute for England, he played his first full game against the Czechs and scored in a 4-2 victory.

An outburst of emotion after being harshly booked against West Germany won the hearts of the nation.

Gazza was an automatic choice for the England squad that competed in the 1990 World Cup Finals in Italy.

New England manager Graham Taylor caused a sensation by leaving Gazza out of the team that played Eire in Dublin.

S YOUR
YOUR
LIFE

se
der

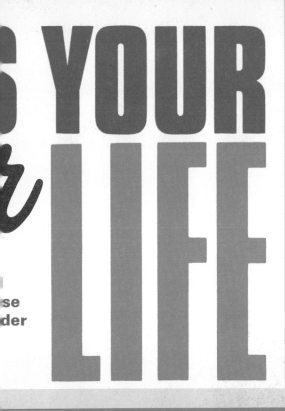

One of the highlights of the
1990-91 season was Gazza's goal
from a free-kick against Arsenal in
the FA Cup Semi-Final at Wembley.
A few weeks later, a serious injury
in the Cup Final disrupted an £8.5
million move to Lazio and a new
life in Rome.

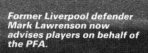

Former Liverpool defender Mark Lawrenson now advises players on behalf of the PFA.

Gordon Taylor: Powerful voice.

PROFESSIONAL FOOTBALLERS ASSOCIATION

Broth

It costs less than 50 pence per week for footballers to buy an inspirational mind, a sympathetic ear, a comforting shoulder and a powerful voice.

Little wonder that 99.9 per cent of players invest in a £25 a year membership to the Professional Footballers' Association – the union packed with strikers who never strike.

The PFA has come a long way since it was formed in 1907 to represent the interests of those people lucky enough to make their living playing the beautiful game.

But while a select few are able to secure their futures for life by making a million – or more – from the game, the PFA never forgets its responsibility to the vast majority

who can often en
of bad advice and
planning.

For their £25, p
a whole range of
services, includin
contracts, pensio
education.

The vast major
school without q
that is something
when it comes to
civvy street once
boots.

But if a footbal
into further educa
75 per cent towa
obtaining a degre
certificate.

But perhaps th
player can make
of a new service
1990 – the PFA's

"Footballers can be easy prey and sometimes they are taken for a ride. And we decided to provide this service only after receiving a number of complaints from players regarding certain agents.

"We offer an very attractive alternative because a players agent will take 20 per cent of a players signing on fee after negotiating on their behalf. Our fee works out something like 0.5 per cent."

The PFA has a union representative at each club – a sort of shop steward – to act as a link between players, management and the union. And a handful of them are members of the PFA's management committee.

Chaired by Marwood, the members are Gordon Taylor (chief executive), Brendan Batson (assistant chief executive), Gary Mabbutt, George Berry, Lawrie Sanchez, Clive Baker, Colin Gibson, Pat Nevin and Geoff Twentyman.

Rumours sometimes spread of union reps who fall foul of their club managers simply by carrying out their PFA duties, but Marwood says: "I would like to think that is not the case and I don't know of any instances where a player has stepped down as union rep because he feared it was getting him into trouble with his manager.

"Club bosses are beginning to accept the strength of the PFA, and we get a lot of managers phoning up for advice on things like how much they should fine players for certain offences.

"As a union we try to be as

Chairman Brian Marwood says of the PFA: "We avoid the stereotype image of unions. There are no Arthur Scargill types here."

responsible as we possibly can and try to avoid the stereotype image of unions. There are no Arthur Scargills here and to my knowledge there has never been a strike by players."

But that's not to say the union are afraid of standing up for their members.

Take the case of a young professional at Sheffield Wednesday who, because of uneducated advice of a trainer, was made to do exercises that caused irreparable damage. The player, Andrew Kiwomya, had to retire from football aged 19.

The union took up his case and brought legal proceedings against the Yorkshire club. Finally, after three years of costly legal ping-pong, the union agreed a £25,000 out of court settlement with the club for Kiwomya.

You've all seen the pictures of the PFA's glamorous Player of the Year awards dinner. But if you thought that was all the union was about, now you know better.

Not bad for 60 pence a week.

boots
The PFA – packed with strikers who never strike

RUSHIE'S SIX

▲ MARK HUGHES

Sparky just has to be up there in my top six. He's the strongest person on the ball I have ever seen – you simply can't get the ball off him if you try to match power with power. The only chance a defender has is to try and nick it off his toe.

His close control is brilliant, and I've seen him hold off two or three defenders at once.

The only problem with my Welsh team-mate is he doesn't score enough goals, as I'm sure he would admit. He's famous for those blockbuster volleys yet he doesn't like hitting the net from two or three yards. If he went for more tap ins he would be among the top two or three in the world.

GARY LINEKER ▼

He's totally the opposite to Sparky in as much as the tap ins are his speciality, and those goals are the hallmark of a great forward.

Not many of his goals would win awards but he deserves all the accolades he gets for being able to be in the right place at the right time. A priceless gift, as his bank balance almost certainly testifies.

OF THE BEST

HUGO SANCHEZ ▶

The Mexican has been my favourite forward for a number of years now, because of the terrific job he did for Spanish giants Real Madrid. He's been the leading goalscorer in Spain consistently, hitting an average of 25-30 goals a season, and that's some going in Spain.

But what I like most about him is the work he puts in off the ball – something that isn't always appreciated by everyone who watches football. The man never stands still. He's looking for space all the time – even when his opponents are taking a corner.

And he is deadly inside the box, scoring fantastic goals before celebrating them with a somersault. A terrific player with a lot of style. I've learned a lot from watching Hugo.

▲ CARECA

I thought he was the best player in Italy during my season with Juventus. And he proved during Italia 90 that he is still an excellent striker, even if he didn't score as many goals as he should have done with Brazil.

Diego Maradona took most of the credit during Napoli's brief domination of the Italian League a couple of years back, but Careca was just as influential. A cracking striker.

▲ MARCO VAN BASTEN

The Dutchman isn't far behind Hugo as the best in my book. He's so strong and is another striker who scores spectacular goals.

In many ways he is the complete centre forward and, you know what, he's a nice bloke too. We became friends when I played in Italy a couple of years back.

▼ JURGEN KLINNSMAN

There's only one thing about the German that I don't like, and that's the way he often looks for penalties. He gives blokes like us a bad name.

And that's a shame because he's got a lot going for him. He's very quick, strong, and isn't afraid to shoot. And, just as importantly, he is a good team player, as he has proved both at international level and during club matches with Inter.

SPOTLIGHT ON CRYSTAL

STAN'S THE MAN

Stan Collymore is Palace's latest import from the world of non-League football.

The big striker moved to Selhurst Park from Stafford Rangers for £100,000 last January.

A series of impressive performances for the reserves earned him a first-team chance and he made his debut as a substitute against QPR in February.

He knows it won't be easy to command a regular place in the team and says: "There are a lot of quality strikers at the club and I just have to be patient.

"But Steve Coppell didn't put me under pressure and told me he didn't expect anything of me until I gained some League experience.

"He wanted me to get a good pre-season behind me and take it from there. Hopefully I'm not letting him down."

WRIGHT WAY TO THE TOP

The continuing success story of Ian Wright (left) should give hope to all up and coming footballers.

Just five years ago, Wright was playing Sunday League football but he is now one of the most feared strikers in the First Division and an England international.

Wright made his full England debut against Cameroon last February, and became only Palace's fourth post-war England international.

And Wright was within inches of making it a dream debut on that freezing February night.

Gary Lineker scored twice in England's 2-0 win but Wright was so close to capping his first appearance with a goal.

He was closing in on John Barnes' right wing corner but Lineker nipped in before him to apply the finishing touch.

But Wright says: "It would have been marvellous to have scored but it was a dream come true simply to play for England."

For the record, Palace's other post-war England stars were: Johnny Byrne, Peter Taylor and Kenny Sansom.

PALACE

TWIN PEAKS

Thorn and Young are a tower of strength

Ian Wright and Mark Bright are generally the players who grab the headlines for Palace.

But they would be the first to admit that they couldn't do their job without the rest of the team.

And two of their team-mates who have done more than most to help them are Andy Thorn (right) and Eric Young.

The reason is simple: Palace no-longer need to rely on their star strikers to score a hatful of goals because Thorn and Young, along with 'keeper Nigel Martyn, make sure that the opposition don't score many either.

Thorn and Young (left) are former Wimbledon team-mates and they helped the unfashionable South London club to win the FA Cup in 1988.

And the two defensive giants are now doing a similar job for The Eagles.

Manager Steve Coppell admits: "Just to see those two standing there fills the team with confidence."

Thorn was already at the club when Coppell paid Wimbledon £850,000 to take Young to Selhurst Park.

He says: "I paid more than I wanted for Eric but I had to sign a tried and trusted player.

"The two of them complement each other well and they've played a big part in our success."

ON A WING AND A PRAYER

John Salako (right) takes an unusual item of kit with him to matches – his bible.

The flying winger is a born-again Christian who now puts his faith right up there alongside his football.

Salako is part of a growing number of footballers who have found God.

Others include Glenn Hoddle and Cyrille Regis.

Salako discovered religion through former team-mate Dennis Bailey. "He is a devout Christian and we used to room together on away trips," says Salako.

"I started going to Church with him and my commitment developed from there. We belong to an organisation called Christians in Sport."

He wears a gold crucifix around his neck and will always be seen crossing himself and saying a prayer before matches.

The striker continues: "Over the past couple of years I have found more and more players turning to religion.

"I get ribbed by the other lads at the club but there is nothing vicious about it."

CRUIS

KERRY'S GOAL

Chelsea striker Kerry Dixon is poised to break a long standing club record this season.

Bobby Tambling scored 202 goals in all competitions for Chelsea in eleven years before joining Crystal Palace in 1969 and Dixon is now within sight of that total.

He says: "It's one of my main aims to beat that tally and do something that no other forward at this club will have done.

"I still have three years left on my contract so I have plenty of time providing I avoid injury."

CRUISE DESK AWARDS 1991

Introducing the first (and probably the last!) Cruise Desk Awards. The winners' prizes are in the post ... honestly.

Player of the Year: Gordon Strachan (Leeds) (above)
Manager of the Year: Dave Bassett (Sheffield United)
Team of the Year: Arsenal
Goal of the Season: Gazza's free-kick v Arsenal (FA Cup Semi-Final)
Game of the Season: Leeds 4 Liverpool 5
Wally of the Year: Diego Maradona for his drug-taking exploits.
Cock-up of the Year: Keith Hackett's decision to send-off West Ham's Tony Gale during the FA Cup Semi-Final against Nottingham Forest.
Diplomat of the Year: Billy Bonds for his after-match reaction to the above incident.
Supporters of the Year: West Ham's for the sporting way they accepted defeat in the above game.
Haircut of the Year: Howard Gayle (Blackburn)

What's the difference between a football club manager and a football club coach?

Well, when Crystal Palace coach Ian Branfoot (left) was asked that question by a football reporter last season he pondered for a few seconds before replying: "About 30 grand a year!"

Napoli were awarded three penalties in one match last season when they beat Parma 4-2. The referee was Roberto Lo Bello.

The last time Napoli were awarded three spot-kicks in a game was 26 years ago. The referee that day was Concetto Lo Bello – Roberto's father! Watch this space in 26 years time!

back. So, to make them really suffer, I've produced a witty and humorous Annual special. Hope you enjoy it.

DESK

SUB-STANDARD

Have you ever been to watch a match and missed a substitution? Or seen the player go off but not recognised him?

Like me, I'm sure you have and in those cases the fans rely on the club announcer to give them the details.

Well, spare a thought for supporters of Hamilton Academicals. Their groundsman, Willie McInnes, used to make such announcements and once gave them this classic description of a substitution: "The man coming on is replacing the man coming off!"

CURRYING FAVOUR

The life of a football reporter can be hazardous as one Northern scribe found out last season.

Whilst visiting Darlington one day, the club he covered for the local paper, he overheard manager Brian Little shout: "I want Currie."

So the next day, the back page story focused on Darlington's attempts to sign their former star striker David Currie from Barnsley.

Unfortunately for the reporter in question, Little's request had more to do with his stomach than football.

The actual remark was made to a young apprentice who was about to go and fetch the manager's lunch. His order: a CURRY.

A lovely story reached me from Merseyside last season. This is how it goes.

Some years ago, football fan Gordon Lee set off to watch Grimsby play a Cup-tie at Liverpool. The crowd was expected to top 45,000 and Gordon didn't want to be late.

After he had left, his wife noticed two neighbours getting into their car also to travel to Anfield.

"Are you going to Liverpool?" she enquired. They nodded.

"Then will you give Gordon his flask. He forgot it," she asked.

The two men looked at each other in amazement before one said: "If we see him, we'll buy him a cup of tea."

Needless to say, they didn't find him.

Don't worry...be happy

Supporters of perennial strugglers such as Halifax, Aldershot and Rochdale can relax for another season.

The constant fear for supporters of Fourth Division clubs in the last few years has been that their team would finish bottom of the Football League, and therefore be relegated to the GM Vauxhall Conference.

But this season, as last, there will be no relegation from the Fourth Division.

One team will be promoted to the Conference, extending the number of League clubs to 94.

But be warned. From next season, 1992-93, the old system of one up and one down will be re-introduced.

Did you hear the one about the burglar and the football team? No, well this is how it goes.

Gainsborough Trinity were returning home from an HFS Loans League game against Chorley towards the end of last season when they spotted a burglar darting across the rooftops, before taking to his heels down the road.

The law abiding Trinity players set off in pursuit of him, firstly in the coach, and then on foot.

The players finally apprehended him down an alley, much to the delight of the local police.

Well done Trinity.

THE BEST (AND WORST) OF CRUISE DESK 1991

Predicting the future can be a tricky task as I found out to my cost last season.

I started off well enough by predicting that not only would Vinny Jones (below) leave Leeds, but that he would team up again with his old boss Dave Bassett at Sheffield United.

So, an early success and I was feeling confident.

But after that initial boost I was to go into decline for a while.

My hot tip that Steve Bruce would rejoin Norwich (one of my learned colleagues assured me that would happen) ended up looking as likely as Derby avoiding relegation.

And talking of Derby, we came up with the news that Paul Goddard was set to rejoin them from Millwall. Well, we all make mistakes.

But there were further successes. SHOOT readers were the first to know that Bryan Robson was set to stay at Manchester United. And sure enough he signed a new two-year contract.

And just to prove that we've got our ears to the ground North of the border as well, we announced that Hibernian star Paul Kane would join Oldham. And he did.

All in all, not a bad effort I thought.

STAI
STR

Grid-Iron giants London Monarchs aren't the only Americans to have tasted Wembley glory recently. Sheffield Wednesday star John Harkes crossed the Atlantic via Seoul and Italy to play a vital role in The Owls' Rumbelows Cup Final win over Manchester United last season.

And that Wembley success was just another chapter in the remarkable rise to stardom of the 25-year-old defender.

"I can't believe how quickly my career has taken off," says John.

"I was part of the US national side that took part in the 1988

ARKES IS A...

IN
PES

Olympics in South Korea, then I played in the World Cup finals in Italy. They were both memorable occasions but playing in a Cup Final at Wembley was even more of a dream come true."

Harkes was close to joining Blackburn and Celtic before opting for Wednesday following a trial at the club.

"It's always been my ambition to play for a top club over here," he says. "I'd hoped to make it much earlier than I did.

"I was only on a temporary contract after the World Cup but kept battling away in the reserves until I got my first team break – and a permanent contract."

The roller-coaster ride to success didn't end there for the star in stripes as he helped Wednesday win promotion to the First Division at the first attempt to complete a double triumph for the Hillsborough club.

And John's even come up trumps with a taste of home bang in the middle of Sheffield in the form of an American diner.

Harkes, son of Scottish parents (his dad played for Dundee reserves) can tuck in to a Hamburger American style and rub shoulders with the Statue of Liberty.

"The diner gives me a feel of home. The whole lifestyle thing was hard to come to terms with at first," he says. "It was all so different but now I'm loving every minute of it here."

EOIN SKIPS TO IT

SUPPORTERS had to look twice as they caught a glimpse of the fresh-faced youngster helping to load the team skip on to the bus.

Could this really be the player who had dazzled the crowd by grabbing all four goals in his side's 4-1 thrashing of Dunfermline last season?

There was no time for Aberdeen scoring sensation Eoin Jess to get carried away with his success. "The boss keeps telling me to keep my feet on the ground," he smiled. "The skip is part of my job as well."

That one-man demolition job at East End Park underlined the young striker's enormous potential and took him to the top of Scotland's scoring chart, ahead of experienced rivals like Mo Johnston and Ally McCoist.

"I'd never managed four in a game before, not even for the reserves," he pointed out. "It was just like a dream, although I felt I might have scored a fifth before the end."

No wonder Dons manager Alex Smith is raving about the latest talented youngster to climb off the Pittodrie conveyor belt. "He can go all the way to the very top," he enthused.

But Eoin's scoring exploits are causing more than a little embarrassment at Ibrox. You see, he was once on schoolboy forms with Rangers and they decided against taking up their option on him.

Aberdeen-born Eoin was only too pleased to accept the offer to join his local side and within two years he was making his senior debut at the age of 18.

Boss Smith reckons Eoin has all the attributes of a top-class striker. "His ability to control the ball with either foot is a great asset and he can turn either way," explained Smith.

"He is very well balanced and his strength and pace will improve as he gets more games under his belt. Like all good strikers, he has an eye for goal and you can see the kick he gets out of sticking the ball in the net."

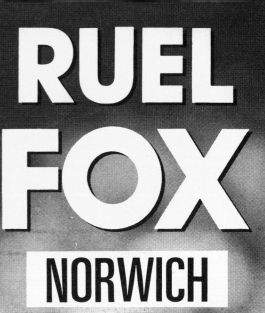

RUEL FOX

NORWICH

NO DOUBT most of you will have your own particular soccer heroes like Paul Gascoigne, Gary Lineker and Marco Van Basten. Now here's your chance to discover the players some of today's stars idolise.

Dean **Saunders**
(Derby County)

I used to model myself on Welsh striker Alan Curtis, who played for my hometown club Swansea City during the 1970s. I also admire players with great individual skills, with the ability to do the unusual. Maradona, Hagi, and Paul Gascoigne are among my present day favourites, I'd queue up and pay to watch them play any day.

Paul **Gascoigne**
(England)

The player I rate above all other is my old Newcastle team mate Glenn Roeder. His foot over the ball trick is brilliant. We became very close while Glenn was at St James' Park and I see a great deal of him now he's back at Watford.

David **Seaman**
(Arsenal)

Like many people inside and out of the game I'm a great Gazza fan. He can do things that other players can only dream about. But when I was a kid, Tony Currie and David Harvey were the biggest influences on me, mainly because they were playing for my team, Leeds United during the 1970s.

Ian **Bishop**
(West Ham)

I was only five-years-old when I watched my hero Charlie George in action for the first time. I'll never forget the day when Charlie scored the FA Cup winner for Arsenal against Liverpool in 1971. From that golden moment I followed Charlie's career until he retired. My idol of recent years is former Spurs and England midfielder Glenn Hoddle. I would pay to watch him train!

HERO

Ian Crook (Norwich City)

My hero was West Ham and England midfield star Trevor Brooking. Brilliant on the field, a real sportsman who was a fine ambassador for the game. Today I love watching and playing against Gazza. Not only has he tremendous skill, but he's a great showman.

Kevin Keegan (former England captain)

As a kid I used to stand behind the goal at Doncaster Rovers watching Willie Nimmo in 1957. He was my hero. I thought he was great because I wanted to be a goalkeeper at the time. Just before each game he used to kick both goalposts, it was his ritual and I was fascinated by it and used to look for it before every game. But George Best is the only player I would ever call a genius. He had it all, and more.

Paul McGee (Wimbledon)

My boyhood idol was the Crystal Palace boss Steve Coppell during his successful days as a winger at Manchester United. He had great skill and was so exciting to watch. Of the present players the one I enjoy watching more than most is World Cup star Lothar Matthaus.

Gary Gillespie (Liverpool)

The finest player of any decade for me was the flying Dutchman Johan Cruyff. Even though he played alongside some of the greatest names in world football for Ajax and Holland during the 1970s, Cruyff stood out above the rest. The nearest you'd find to the complete player today is John Barnes. Not only is he a superb player, he's a really nice guy as well.

Not a lotta know that

AN UNUSUAL CLAUSE IN *TORQUAY UNITED'S* LEASE OF THEIR GROUND, STATES THAT 'IT SHOULD ALWAYS BE OPEN TO MEMBERS OF THE GENERAL PUBLIC FOR RECREATION..'

SO IN THEORY ANYONE CAN WALK ACROSS THE PITCH WHENEVER THEY LIKE!

WOLVERHAMPTON WANDERERS ARE THE ONLY CLUB TO HAVE WON THE *CHAMPIONSHIPS* OF ALL FOUR DIVISIONS OF THE FOOTBALL LEAGUE!

CHAMPIONS!

WOLVERHAMPTON WANDERERS. F. C. 1953-
FOOTBALL LEAGUE DIVISION. I-CHAMPIONS

fans

...

OVER 20,000 WORDS FOR ONE MATCH REPORT, MUST BE SOMETHING OF A WORLD RECORD! THIS REPORT WAS SENT BACK TO THE ARGENTINE BY ONE OF THEIR REPORTERS AT THE WORLD CUP FINALS HERE IN 1966!

PORT VALE'S RIGHT MIDFIELDER DURING THE 1952-53 SEASON WAS THE LOCAL VICAR!

BURNLEY WERE THE FIRST FOOTBALL LEAGUE CLUB TO BE VISITED BY ROYALTY WHEN *PRINCE ALBERT* VISITED THEIR GROUND IN 1886. THEY ALSO APPEARED IN THE FIRST CUP FINAL TO BE ATTENDED BY ROYALTY IN 1914.

SOCCASTATS

YORKE'S FAN CLUB

DWIGHT YORKE, Aston Villa's teenage striker, may not be a household name in Britain just yet, but it's a different story in his native Trinidad and Tobago.

Yorke, plucked from the Caribbean by former Villa boss Graham Taylor, cannot walk down the street in Tobago without being mobbed by groups of fans.

He is rapidly developing a cult status in his homeland as he bids to earn a regular place in the first-team at Villa Park.

He says: "It is nice to know that the people at home are so interested in me, but sometimes there is not enough privacy when you are in the limelight.

"Obviously, that does not happen so much in England, but when I go home I am likely to be mobbed by fans.

"I have to say that it is quite nice in one way, but sometimes it gets you down because you have to be so careful in everything you do.

"I know that if I was playing regular first-team football, the TV people at home would be trying to get something from the games on telly and everyone would be looking out for me."

Yorke, who won 20 international caps by the time he was 18, has ambitious plans to help Trinidad and Tobago qualify for the 1994 World Cup in America after they narrowly failed to earn a spot in Italy.

They were beaten in their final qualifying game by the USA, but Yorke is determined that they will go one better in qualifying next time.

However, he knows that his main priority at the moment is a regular place in the Villa first-team.

He is a third of the way through a three-year contract at Villa Park and made his full first-team debut for Villa against Manchester United at Old Trafford last season.

He says: "Of course I am interested in playing for my country, but at the moment I should concentrate on my football in England as this is where my career lies at the moment.

"The football here is ever so competitive. I quite like the style, but sometimes I think that the pace is too fast."

FOOTBALL FUNNIES

"Three men booked – one sent-off – two injured – we lost 10-nil – and you have the audacity to call that a slight hiccup"

"Our superstar has a sort of injury fixation – you name it, he's had it"

"But think for a moment ... how would it look in the papers? Chairman shoots manager"

"I didn't mean what I said about your eyesight, ref"

"I bet you miss playing football on a Saturday, Mr. Brown"

"No darling, daddy isn't in pain. He's practising a few moves for tomorrow's Cup-tie"

23

I ENJOY SEEING HAMMERS BEATEN!

SENSATION!

reveals Alf Garnett, West Ham's greatest 'fan'

YOU never know who you are going to see at a football match. As well as the stars on the pitch there are also stars to be seen in the grandstand.

During the 1990 World Cup in Italy Luciano Pavarotti did more than bring some vocal culture to the game. His unmistakable frame could be seen at many of Italy's matches as he roared his country on in their quest for glory.

On any Saturday afternoon in the English Football League you can rub shoulders with other stars, just as keen on their favourite clubs.

Perhaps the best known is the support for West Ham by actors Nick Berry and Leslie Grantham who made no secret of the fact when they were both behind the bar of the Queen Vic pub in EastEnders as Simon Wicks and Den Watts respectively.

A Hammers scarf could always be seen behind the bar in those days. Leslie Grantham left Albert Square to take up residence at the Paradise Club, but he is still a regular at Upton Park.

Another well-known Hammers 'fan' wouldn't give you much thanks for a season ticket to Upton Park. He is Warren Mitchell. In his

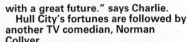

famous role as Alf Garnett he unceasingly sings the praises of The Hammers. In real life, Warren Mitchell is a devoted Spurs fan and rarely misses a game at White Hart Lane.

"I've always followed Spurs," says Warren. "The only time you'd get me to Upton Park would be to see West Ham beaten at home by Spurs. Alf doesn't know what he's talking about."

And Spurs have another fan, or rather a whole collection of them wrapped up in the form of Bobby Davro, ace impersonator who can be almost anyone from Ben Elton to Elton John. Even as Elton John he will follow Spurs.

"There's only ever been Spurs for me. There's nobody in the same class," says Bobby.

"I think Arsenal are great," says Gary Wilmot, also backed up by a team of his well-known impersonation characters. "I have followed The Gunners since I was a kid. They have had some great teams but today's side would take some beating."

Another Arsenal fan is Peter Dean, EastEnders' Peter Beale.

"I don't live very far from Highbury and go to see them when I can. I think they are the best team in the country. I'm looking forward to seeing them in Europe."

Away from London, Aston Villa's top supporter is pop violinist Nigel Kennedy.

"I hardly ever miss a game. I've supported them since I was little and I travel all over the place to see them including away matches abroad," says Nigel.

TV comedian Charlie Daze also follows Villa.

"I used to be a pro player myself when I was in Ireland. I played for Portadown. I love the game. I had the chance to play in the Football League but an injury stopped me. What I like about Villa is that you can take your

Gary Glitter has supported many teams.

family there without any problems and they can play some great football."

Another comedian, Charlie Williams actually did play in the Football League for Barnsley. He still lives near the club and follows their progress.

"We'll be in the First Division before long and then there'll be no stopping Barnsley. It's a great club with a great future." says Charlie.

Hull City's fortunes are followed by another TV comedian, Norman Collyer.

"I still live in Hull and I have been going to Boothferry Park since I can remember. Things have taken a bit of a dive recently, but The Tigers will be back."

Those thoughts are echoed by the pop band the House Martins who also come from Hull and still go to see The Tigers as often as they are able.

Rod Stewart, no mean footballer himself, keeps a keen eye on Crewe as well as Celtic, Aberdeen and Manchester United.

"I've got a special soft spot for Crewe. United and Celtic are two of the greatest clubs in the world and Aberdeen is where I was born so that's why I follow all of them," Rod explained.

Still in the pop world, Eddie Grant

Pop star Rod Stewart keeps an eye on Crewe.

is also a keen footballer and follows West Ham, while Gary Glitter cannot make up his mind.

"I move house a lot and I like to follow my local team. In recent seasons I have supported Oxford, Bristol City, Bristol Rovers and Chelsea. The trouble is that once you start to follow a team you can never stop. By the time I have finished I will probably have supported every club in the League," says Gary.

Jess Conrad runs the Showbix XI football team and has raised millions of pounds for charities.

"I go to either Highbury or White Hart Lane for matches," says Jess. "I'd better not say which I prefer as they might ban me from the other one."

In the North, Ken Dodd will have nothing said against Liverpool.

"Second only to Diddyland Rovers, Liverpool are the greatest team in the history of football," says Doddy. "If you don't believe me, ask any Everton supporter, they'll tell you how great Liverpool are."

Stan Boardman and Jimmy Tarbuck will go along with that. Stan is perhaps the greatest fan of all.

Gary Wilmot (inset) is an Arsenal fanatic.

CONTINUED OVER

"Nobody to touch them," he says. "I was brought up a Liverpool fan and I could never imagine following anyone else, except England, of course.

"If I'm away doing a show I make sure I have a radio in the dressing-room so that I don't miss anything."

Doesn't anyone follow Everton?

"I do," says Frank Carson. "I live in Blackpool so I follow my local side but I think Everton are great and Howard Kendall is a great manager – it's the way he tells —em."

Bullseye host Jim Bowen is another comedian who can't help keeping a radio with him.

"I've always got the car radio on if I'm away on a Saturday afternoon. Blackburn Rovers are my team and I can't wait to see them back in the First Division. Last season was a bit of a disappointment but just wait till next year."

Another comedian, Eddie Large has been a life-long follower of Manchester City and he goes to Maine Road as often as possible.

"Give us another season or two and we'll be Champions

Ken Dodd.

again," says Eddie. "It's a great club and we're going back to the top where we belong."

Echoing that thought is Kevin Kennedy, perhaps better known as Curly Watts of Coronation Street. He is also a City fan and has a friendly rivalry with fellow street star Michael Le Vel who plays Kevin Webster. Michael is a United fan.

"I go to Old Trafford a lot. I always have done. It's the greatest club in the world. We have a lot of leg-pulling on a Monday if United have won and City have lost. If it's the other way round I dread going into work.

"I live near Oldham and I go to Boundary Park sometimes. You see some good football there."

Other famous names have been linked with Oldham, now back in the First Division. Eric Sykes was on the board for some time and former Rochdale chairman Tommy Cannon comes from there.

"Bobby Ball and I come from Oldham and I have never stopped watching their results. I go to see them whenever I get the chance," says Tommy.

Rochdale meanwhile have a firm fan in Jimmy Cricket.

"I lived in Rochdale for years. You can't help liking the club. Anyway they are nearer than my home team of Ballygobackwards. I used to play for Ballygobackwards Wednesday. Everyone else played Saturday," Jimmy explains.

But if one club can consider itself to be a cut above the rest it has to be Chelsea. Every week a whole host of famous names can be seen at Stamford Bridge with Prime Minister, John Major, topping the poll of celebrities.

"It's not so easy to get to the Bridge these days but I'll continue to go when I can. I always keep track of what is going on by television and radio. There's no greater game than football and I like to think there's no greater club than Chelsea," says Mr Major.

So keep your eyes open when you go to soccer matches, you are rubbing shoulders with the stars.

Cannon and Ball go to Oldham (below) when showbiz commitments allow.

MAURICE Football Focus MALPAS

Date of birth: August 3,1962 …
Married: Yes, to Marina …
Children: A son Darren (5) and a daughter 1-year-old Zoe …
House: A three-bedroomed bungalow in Monifeith … Car: A VW Passat.

When was your senior debut? A few months into the 1981-82 season against Airdrie. My most vivid memory is how easy we managed to win. The result was 4-0.

What is your most memorable game? When we beat Dundee at Dens Park to win the League Championship in 1983. Ralph Milne scored a beauty with a chip from 25 yards and our fans were jubilant after the game.

What is the best game you have ever seen? Kenny Dalglish's final game in charge for Liverpool – the 4-4 FA Cup-tie against Everton. It was an amazing game with some incredible goals.

Which school did you attend? Queen Anne High School in Dunfermline, where I gained 6 O levels and 5 highers. After that I went to college and gained an Honours Degree in Electric and Electronic Engineering, and for the first five years at United I was a part-timer.

Which player did you idolise as a boy? I was a Leeds United fan and Billy Bremner was my favourite player. A wee man with a big heart.

Who do you look like? People keep telling me I look like Jimmy White, and I keep telling them I play snooker like him too. I smash the balls around the table.

What is your favourite film? I've watched Stir Crazy, starring Richard Pryor and Gene Wilder, over and over again and it still makes me laugh. Sea of Love is another favourite, though I can't remember who's in that.

And your favourite book? Anything about golf.

Who is your favourite musician? Phil Collins. In my younger years I was a Genesis fan and I've followed Phil's career ever since.

What is the most outrageous item of clothing in your wardrobe? There are a couple of wild jerseys, one multi-coloured one that caused a lot of laughs among the United lads. It's horrendous

DUNDEE UNITED AND SCOTLAND

really but it was a present from my mother-in-law so I have to wear it.

What was your most embarrassing moment in football? During a testimonial match for

Mark Walters.

Paul Hegarty I actually threatened to score a goal. I sold the 'keeper a beautiful dummy but then kicked the ground and fluffed my shot from the 6 yard line.

What is your idea of a perfect day off? A round of golf and then some time with my family.

Who is the most boring player at your club? You're going to get me into trouble. Hamish French is the quietest member of the squad.

Who is your toughest opponent? Davie Cooper has given me a few problems over the years. He is such a good player on the ball and can make an opponent look a bit silly at times.

What is the weakest element of your game? My crossing – but I'm working on it.

Which player would you pay to watch? Someone who tries to entertain as well as win. Someone like Mark Walters or Paul Gascoigne.

Which nation will win the European Championships in Sweden? Italy. I don't think they did themselves justice during the World Cup and I think they will be determined to put that right.

BONNER'S WORLD

BOOST

WHAT a difference international stardom can make to a player. Take the case of Pat Bonner, the amiable Celtic goalkeeper whose World Cup performances for the Republic of Ireland last summer have provoked a number of enviable spin-offs.

His fan mail – the bulk of which comprises requests for autographed photographs and children presenting him with their drawings of his penalty save against Romania – currently stands at 100 letters a week.

In his home country, he is featured in a major advertising campaign for a building society and is in great demand for public appearances.

His fame has helped him as a player, too.

Tommy Craig, the Celtic coach, feels that Bonner's World Cup performances, and the status he has gained because of them, has helped him become more relaxed and self-confident.

Pressure

Bonner agrees. "It is a lovely feeling to know that you are so appreciated by your own people," he says.

One way in which he has been helped by this is that it has made him more composed under pressure.

Packy has a fiery temperament, which was particularly pronounced in his early days with Celtic. His first Celtic coach, Frank Connor, once a goalkeeper himself, felt this was the only factor which might prevent Bonner reaching the top.

"I still tend to get a bit uptight," Bonner admits, "but the experience of playing in the European Championship and the World Cup has definitely helped me take things in my stride a bit more."

Bonner, who joined Celtic in 1978, at the age of 18, has spared nothing in his bid to fulfilling his potential.

An indication of his approach can be found in a red folder bulging with notes he has written on goalkeeper techniques and training ideas.

Tommy Craig uses them as a guide when working with him, because as Bonner says: "It is difficult for me to

Pat's famous penalty save against Romania.

see faults I might have got into. At the same time, it is important that the person watching me knows what to look for.

"In my own case, I have written down things which I feel apply to me personally, taking into account my physique, my temperament and my natural style. You know, what is right for one keeper might not be right for another."

Because of his build – 6ft 2in, 13st – most of his training is devoted to his sharpness and mobility, his ability to get to low shots close to his body and deep far post crosses.

The latter caused him particular problems at one time. His ability to attack the ball correctly was undermined because he did not anticipate crosses correctly, and was forced to take too many steps to get to the ball.

"It was something that took him

quite some time to master," Craig says. "It is interesting to see him going for crosses these days. As opposed to a little pitter-patter, it is sort of one-two-up."

That, in fact, is the perfect way to describe the way his career – and his life – have gone since the start of the Irish Republic's rise in the world football rankings.

His stature is best illustrated by the change in his relationship with Celtic's manager, Billy McNeill. In Bonner's early days at Parkhead, McNeill was deliberately provocative in his dealings with him.

In striving to make Bonner tougher, mentally, he even instructed other players to knock him about in training.

Now, Bonner, as a player who has proved himself at the highest level, is left to do whatever he feels is right and McNeill often consults him for advice.

ITALIA '90 CREATED A BIG DEMAND FOR THE REPUBLIC OF IRELAND 'KEEPER.

ROBBIE
DENNISON
Wolves

GORDON DURIE

CHELSEA AND SCOTLAND

Date of birth: December 6, 1965 ... Married: Yes, to Sheila ... House: A four bedroomed detached house in Camberley, Surrey ... Car: A Mazda 626.

When was your senior debut?
Two months after my 16th birthday for East Fife in 1982. We drew 1-1 against Stranraer. I didn't get the goal but I managed to score in my second game against Cowdenbeath.

What is your most memorable game?
My debut for Scotland against Bulgaria in a European Championship game almost five years ago. I came on as a substitute and although I only played for 25 minutes it was a special night for me. Gary Mackay scored the only goal of the game.

What is the best game you have ever seen?
West Germany v France during the 1982 World Cup. Real end-to-end stuff between two quality teams.

Which school did you attend?
Inverkeithing High School, where I gained O levels in English, Maths and Modern Studies. Don't ask why I took the last one, I'm still not sure myself.

Which player did you idolise as a boy?
Kenny Dalglish. I was a Rangers fan but Kenny played some brilliant football for Celtic and I would go to Parkhead just to watch him. He didn't have a weakness as a player.

Who do you look like?
Haven't a clue.

What's your favourite book?
I suppose I would have to say Jaws by Peter Benchley. It's the only book I've read.

Who is your favourite musician?
Whitney Houston. I've seen her live a few times and she has got a fantastic voice. A real star.

What is your most outrageous item of clothing?
Nothing too drastic, although there are a couple of wicked multi-coloured ties in my wardrobe.

What is your most embarrassing moment in football?
Getting relegated in 1988 after a play-off match at home to Middlesbrough. We thought we were too good to go down but we were wrong.

Who would you most like to be trapped in a lift with?
I can't answer that – the wife is listening.

What is your idea of a perfect day off?
A long lie in bed and, if there was enough time after that, a supreme round of golf.

Who is the most boring player at your club?
Reserve goalkeeper Roger Freestone. They say goalies are mad but Roger never says a word.

Who is your most difficult opponent?
I would put Mark Wright just ahead of Des Walker. He's commanding and powerful.

What is the weakest element of your game?
Sheila keeps telling me it is my heading so I'll have to say that. But I'm working hard to improve that part of my game and I think it's getting better.

Which player would you pay to watch?
As I've said already I paid to see Dalglish and I've not seen anyone as good as him since.

Who is your tip to win the European Championships in Sweden?
I would like to think Scotland will have a chance but I suppose Germany will be the favourites. England will fancy their chances too, because they are one of the strongest sides.

FORREST SAVED!

GOALKEEPER Craig Forrest got lost on his way to Ipswich, but has long since arrived in the football big-time.

The only Canadian-born player in the Football League, he originally came to England in 1984 on a month's trial – and he's been here ever since.

Apart from establishing himself as number one for Ipswich, the 6ft 5ins goalkeeper has also become first choice for his country and one day hopes to represent Canada in the World Cup Finals.

A lot has happened since Craig, then a 16-year-old hopeful, got lost on the London Underground after flying into Heathrow Airport laden down with four suitcases packed with everything he owned.

"I eventually found my way to Ipswich," he recalls with a grin, "and I've only ever been back to Canada to visit my folks and have a holiday."

Liverpool goalkeeper Bruce Grobbelaar was one of Craig's boyhood heroes. "He played for Vancouver Whitecaps, my local team, and my family had season tickets. I saw all his games out there and I used to dream about following in his footsteps," recalls Craig.

"My main aim is to help Ipswich back into the First Division and then line up against Bruce. He helped me at a couple of coaching clinics back in Vancouver but I doubt if he would remember me now."

Former Ipswich youth player Phil Trenter was responsible for arranging Craig's trial at Portman Road. He worked alongside Craig's father, Lorne, in the Vancouver Fire Department.

Ipswich agreed to take a look at Craig, but insisted he paid his own expenses. "My parents had to come up with the money for the plane fare," he recalls.

Craig served his apprenticeship in the youth and reserve sides before making his League debut while on loan to neighbours Colchester near the end of the 1987-88 campaign.

The following season he took over as first choice for Ipswich and he has been a commanding figure between the sticks ever since.

Not surprisingly, his best friend at Ipswich is fellow Canadian international Frank Yallop, the Watford-born defender who emigrated to Vancouver with his parents when he was a youngster.

ROBERT WARZYCHA

EVERTON

GLORY GLORY MAN UTD

Relive the two Mark Hughes goals that beat Barcelona in Rotterdam to win the European Cup-Winners' Cup for Manchester United in May ... their first European honour since 1968 when they defeated Benfica at Wembley.

Manchester United's Mark Hughes is the only player to have won the PFA Player of the Year Award twice ... in 1989 and '91.

PRIZE GUYS!

There is no finer accolade than being voted an award winner by your fellow professionals ... or people in the game. That's why the Football Writers' Association and Professional Footballers' Association Awards are so highly prized. But so is the Shoot/adidas Golden Shoe which is presented to the leading League goalscorers in each of the four English Divisions and the Scottish Premier. Here is a pictorial tribute to last season's top individualists.

Sparky's United team-mate Lee Sharpe was voted the PFA Young Player of the Year. He was also the Barclays Young Eagle of the Year and won Shoot's Most Exciting English League Player of the Year Award.

Leeds United's Gordon Strachan was narrowly beaten in the voting for the PFA Award. But the FWA Footballer of the Year trophy highlighted a great season and came a few days after his recall to the Scotland team.

Lee Sharpe showing the kind of form that attracted so much attention during a season that ended with three individual trophies and a European Cup-Winners' Cup medal.

Arsenal's sharp-shooter Alan Smith scores against Coventry. He ended the season with 22 First Division goals to win the Shoot/Adidas Golden Shoe Award.

Dundee United's Maurice Malpass failed to land a Scottish Cup winners' medal ... but he was voted Player of the Year.

Eion Jess helped Aberdeen end the season as Championship runners-up. He was also Scotland's Young Player of the Year.

Arsenal won the Barclays League Championship losing just one game, away at Chelsea. George Graham fully justified his Manager of the Year Award.

Tommy Coyne scores for Celtic against Rangers. His 18 Premier League goals won him the Shoot/Adidas Golden Shoe for the second time. He was a winner with Dundee in 1987-88.

Barclays League Winners Arsenal

WE ARE THE CHA

Second Division
Oldham Athletic

Third Division
Cambridge United

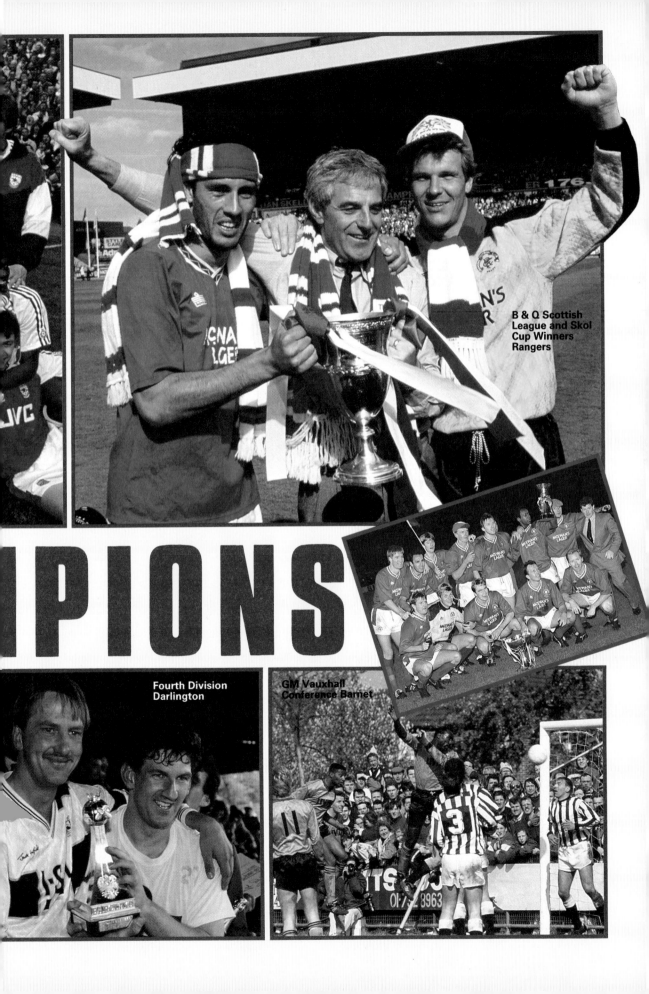

B & Q Scottish League and Skol Cup Winners Rangers

MPIONS

Fourth Division Darlington

GM Vauxhall Conference Barnet

John Sheridan scores the goal that shocked Manchester United and won the 1991 Rumbelows Cup for the underdogs Sheffield Wednesday.

Below: United's brave 'keeper Les Sealey refused to go off despite a horrendous injury.

Wednesday defender Roland Nilsson did a fine job keeping the dangerous Lee Sharpe at bay.

OWLS

THAT!

Wednesday manager Ron Atkinson gets that winning feeling.

Mark Hughes and Nigel Pearson gave no quarter.

Motherwell's victorious captain Tom Boyd (now Chelsea).

Steve Kirk scores the goal that beat Dundee United.

Paul Stewart's superb equaliser for Spurs.

CU
CRAC

Salute to the 1991 FA and Scottish Cup Winners

UP
KERS

Spurs skipper Gary Mabbutt lifts the FA Cup.

Forest's Des Walker heads past his own 'keeper to score Tottenham's winner.

Paul Gascoigne stretchered off after just ten minutes.

Neto is Brazil's best – says Pele

EZIDIO NETO is the man around whom Brazil are building their dreams. He's the sort of attacking midfielder the torcida – Brazil's fans – love.

Neto loves nothing better than turning on a show, indulging in a sleight-of-foot technique which his admirers compare with that of Pele, Didi and Garrincha – stars of the 1958 and 1962 World Cup sides.

The incomparable Pele, no less, calls Neto the "best No 10 in Brazil", and the player thrills whenever he hears or reads descriptions of himself as the "Brazilian Maradona" or the "new Rivelino".

Now 25, he says: "I'm proud to be compared with great players. But that also brings great responsibility. So I work hard at my game. After training I always practice around 80 free-kicks. Then I shut myself away and think about the opposition."

Bounced

Neto's self-confidence has not always endeared him to directors or managers. It's one reason he has bounced from Guarani, to Bangu of Rio, to Sao Paulo FC, to Palmeiras of Rio and now to Corinthians of Sao Paulo.

He was left at home when Brazil's 22-strong squad set off for the 1990 World Cup finals in Italy. But Neto intends to be there in 1994 in the United States – along with other new boys such as Moacyr, Mauricio and Joao Paulo.

Ramon Mendoza

EUROPEAN Cup football has become a bigger money-spinner than ever. But the two clubs who did the most to push it down the road towards a Super

'King' Lamptey

AFRICAN Black Magic was a feature of the World Cup as far back as 1966.

Then the hero of the masses was Silva Eusebio Ferreira. He played for Portugal. But his club, Lisbon giants Benfica, had found him in Mozambique, East Africa. His power-drive shooting earned him nine goals at World Cup '66 and a host of marksmanship titles with Benfica.

At Italia '90 it was Cameroon's Roger Milla who set the crowds alight with his goalscoring impact as a second-half substitute.

Now there is another African name to watch for, not in USA '94 maybe, but beyond that. He's Nii Odartey Lamptey and he plays for Belgian champions Anderlecht.

Lamptey was born on December 10, 1974. He was voted Man of the Match playing for Ghana against Scotland in the opening game of the 1989 World Junior Championship in Scotland. Lamptey remembers the occasion well – not for the way he played but because, after the match, Pele shook his hand.

"That was a glorious moment," says Lamptey. "He has always been my hero. I admire him so much."

Lamptey was already a star back home with Cornerstone FC of Accra. But Europe's spies had been out in force and Anderlecht won the race. Their Nigerian defender, Stephen Keshi, was an influential figure. It was Keshi who smuggled Lamptey out of Africa when the Ghanaian federation refused to release his passport!

Anderlecht sweetened the Ghanaians with a £30,000 'transfer' payment. But they could not play their African jewel immediately. Belgian rules prohibit teams lining up professional players until they are 16. So Lamptey had to wait until December, 1990.

Once in, never forgotten. He is now a star at the club.

The name Nii means 'King'. How appropriate that promises to prove.

SUPER LEAGUE

Silvio Berlusconi

AC Milan (left) and Real Madrid in Euro action

Milan on his business trips and takes the opportunity to swap ideas with Berlusconi.

For the past four years they have envisaged a European Club Super League, much of whose income would be generated by the media and sponsorship sectors in which Berlusconi has multi-million interests.

UEFA, the governing body of European football, grew jumpy. Officials came up with a compromise, which takes effect this season.

Instead of the traditional Quarter-Finals and Semi-Finals, the eight qualified teams will play home and away ties in two mini-leagues. That means any club which reaches the Quarter-Finals is guaranteed six matches instead of a mere two. That can add up to a million-pound difference – and without even reaching the Final!

The teams which top the leagues will enter the Final. But it won't be Ruud Gullit's Milan: they're banned from Europe this term for walking off early against Marseille last spring. And it won't be Madrid; they lost their Spanish crown to Barcelona.

League won't be around to cash in.

Milan and Real Madrid, with ten Champions' Cups between them, are both run by powerful, millionaire presidents with ambitions of world domination.

In the red and black corner, TV mogul Silvio Berlusconi of Milan; in the all-white corner, Ramon Mendoza, the entrepreneur president of Madrid.

The two men are old friends. Mendoza frequently flies through

CONTINUED OVERLEAF

£3,200-A-GAME

ANDONI ZUBIZARRETA, Barcelona's Spain goalkeeper, was furious at missing the Cup-Winners' Cup Final defeat against Manchester United last season.

Zubizarreta (right) was banned after collecting a second yellow card for the season in Barsa's Semi-Final against Juventus.

But it was missing a possible share of the glory which upset him – rather than losing out on the prospect of a huge bonus. After all, Zubizarreta is not short of a peseta or two.

When 'Zubi' joined Barcelona from Bilbao in the summer of 1986 he signed an eight-year contract which guaranteed him a minimum £1.8million – before bonuses. That is the equivalent of £225,000-a-year, or £4,300-a-week, or (given that Barcelona play around 70 matches-a-year) £3,200-a-game.

lucrative transfer to Parma as well as the accolade of Swedish Footballer of the Year.

Sweden flew home under a black cloud. Manager Nordin had barely set his feet back in Stockholm before he was out of the door. Several of the older players followed.

For Brolin, however, the world had opened up. Fellow countryman Nils Liedholm, veteran coach of Milan,

BROLIN'S LAST LAUGH

SWEDEN'S ambitions of winning 'their' European Championship rest on the shoulders of baby-faced Tomas Brolin.

Yet he might never have become the centre-forward who now thrills the fans of Italian club Parma, the fans back home and national manager Tommy Svensson.

Coaches at his first club, GIF Sundsvall, considered he was too long on ambition and too short on physique. When Brolin told them he wanted to play centre-forward they laughed at him.

But the laugh was on them after Brolin quit to join Norrkoping, snatched up their No. 9 shirt and scored seven goals in the opening

eight League games of the following season. National manager Ollie Nordin knew a good centre-forward when he saw one. Nordin called him into the national squad warming up for Italia '90 and, once Brolin was on board, he never looked back.

His debut for Sweden was against Wales, less than two months before the start of the World Cup. Brolin scored twice and then shot two more in a 6-0 thrashing of Finland. He was undisputed leader of the line by the time the Swedes landed in Italy for the finals.

The rest of the team flopped. Not Brolin. He scored Sweden's consolation goal in their initial defeat by Brazil and did enough to earn a

Roma and Fiorentina compared Brolin favourably with 50's star Gunnar Nordahl – Sweden's greatest striker.

A more up-to-date comparison – for their lack of height – was made between Brolin and the sharp-shooting West German centre-forward of the 1970s, Gerd Muller.

But Brolin is a thoroughly modern superstar. Never mind Gunnar Nordahl: he doesn't remember Muller, either.

Brolin says: "History means nothing. When you go out to play, all that matters is today. I just try to do my best."

All Sweden will be relying on just that come next June.

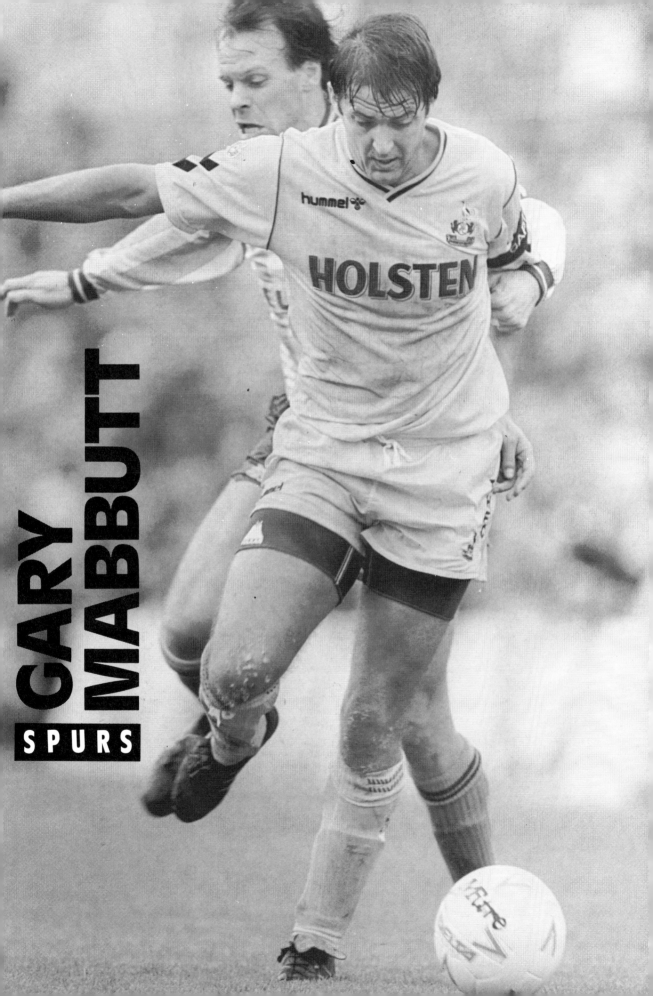

GARY MABBUTT

SPURS

TOPS

Who are England's penalty kings?
A *SHOOT* surveys reveals the
answers and you may well be
surprised at the results.

*Ian Bishop converts a spot-kick
for West Ham at Oldham.*

It has been claimed for years that Liverpool, in particular, benefit from controversial penalty decisions, especially at Anfield.

Indeed, after a match at Anfield in April 1988, Manchester United boss Alex Ferguson raged: "I can understand why clubs come away from here having to bite their tongues knowing they have been done by referees."

But as our table shows, there are other clubs who score even more penalties than Liverpool.

Sheffield United and West Ham tie for first place with 65 converted spot-kicks. (Unfortunately, there are no figures available for the number of penalties awarded.)

Certain aspects need to be taken into consideration when studying the findings of this survey.

For example, many of the teams near the top of the table are lower division clubs. Teams from the Third and Fourth Division are always likely to get more penalties simply because they play more games.

Almost without exception, teams who score nine or ten penalties a season usually end up winning promotion or coming very close.

In the past ten seasons, three teams scored 13 League penalties in a season – Luton in 1981-82 and both Chester and Plymouth in 1985-86. All three were promoted.

However, there are always exceptions. The team who scored most penalties in season 1989-90 were Colchester and they ended up being relegated to the GM Vauxhall Conference!

The table shows that very few of the traditional First Division teams are in the leading positions.

Apart from the fact that lower division teams play more games, this also suggests that they make more clumsy challenges inside the penalty area.

Sheffield United's success is undoubtedly helped by the fact that they have had some good seasons in the past decade – winning promotion four times, though they were relegated twice.

The survey proves that if your team wins a lot of penalties they are most likely to be involved when the season's honours are decided and that Fourth Division games produce the most penalties.

And as for managers who complain about dubious penalty decisions at Anfield, perhaps they should count themselves lucky that they weren't playing at Bramall Lane.

So who scored the most penalties?

NB: Only teams who have completed at least eight of the past 10 seasons in the Football League are included.

Pos.	Pen.	
1	65	Sheffield Utd, West Ham
3	64	Blackpool
4	61	Bradford, Liverpool
6	60	Rotherham
7	59	Portsmouth
8	58	Colchester, Exeter
10	56	Swindon
11	54	Oxford, Sunderland
13	53	Cambridge, Hartlepool, Nottm F., Plymouth, York
18	52	Blackburn, Bury, Chesterfield, Port Vale, Walsall
23	51	Bristol C., Luton, Millwall
26	50	Chelsea, Chester,

POT KICKS

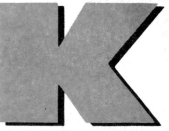
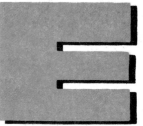

		Northampton, Wigan
30	49	Burnley, Huddersfield, Rochdale
33	48	Everton, Fulham, Leeds, Leicester
37	47	Doncaster
38	46	Grimsby, Scunthorpe
40	45	Newcastle
43	44	Barnsley, Lincoln, Notts Co
46	43	Hull
47	42	C. Palace, Stockport, Swansea
50	41	Preston, Wrexham
52	40	Aston Villa, Darlington, Halifax, Spurs, Watford
57	39	Man City
58	38	Aldershot, Bolton, L. Orient, Man Utd, Mansfield
63	37	Arsenal, Gillingham, Peterborough
66	36	Bournemouth, Brentford, Brighton, Hereford, Oldham, Shrewsbury, Southampton, Wimbledon
75	35	Derby, Southend, Torquay
78	34	Birmingham
79	33	Carlisle, Ipswich, Stoke
82	32	Middlesbrough
83	31	Norwich
84	30	Cardiff, Crewe, QPR, Reading, Sheff Wed, Wolves
90	29	Charlton
91	28	Coventry, Newport
93	27	Bristol R.
94	24	WBA

Arsenal penalty king, Lee Dixon.

PLAYERS THEN MANAGE

Former Everton dynamo Peter Reid ponders his future as manager of Manchester City.

Can you spot what's missing since one-time Wolves star Kenny Hibbitt became manager at Walsall? His beard!

Injury problems forced Glenn Hoddle to quit playing for Monaco and accept the Swindon hot-seat.

The popular Ossie Ardiles has a tough task trying to bring back the glory days to Newcastle United.

Scotland giant Joe Jordan returned North of the border to take over at Hearts.

Billy Bonds has served West Ham as player and manager for 25 years.

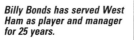

1 During a League match the crossbar is cracked and could be dangerous. Do you (a) play on without a crossbar, (b) improvise with a rope or (c) abandon the match?

2 You see a defender intentionally trip an opponent in the penalty area and award a penalty. However, a neutral linesman says the opponent fell over the defender's leg. Do you (a) insist on a penalty, (b) restart with a drop ball or (c) caution the linesman?

YOU ARE

3 A player collides heavily with a team-mate, but in retaliation he strikes an opponent by mistake. After sending him off do you restart with (a) a drop ball, (b) an indirect or (c) direct free-kick?

4 You are cautioning a goalkeeper for time-wasting when he deliberately pushes an opponent with the ball. Do you (a) is a second caution to the 'keeper, (b) order him off or (c) awa penalty instead of an indirect free-kick?

5

A: From the kick-off the ball is kicked directly into the opposing goal. You disallow the goal and award a goal-kick.

B: The goalkeeper quickly rolls the ball to a team-mate, who is outside the penalty-area and collects it from the return pass.

C: Rolling the ball to the edge of the penalty-area, the 'keeper is about to kick when he is charged fairly by an attacker. He does not release the ball when falling outside the area. You award a free-kick against the 'keeper.
(Where is the problem?)

ANSWERS

1. The match must be abandoned (c) if the crossbar cannot be repaired or replaced with another (Law 1, decision B). 2. (a) Having seen the incident you are not required to consider an alternative opinion of a neutral linesman. The penalty-kick must stand. 3. A direct free-kick (c) is the correct decision. 4. Any player (b) who is being cautioned then comm'its another cautionable offence must be sent off (Law 12, decision 13). 5 The problem is in B. The ball must be kicked from a goal-kick, it should be retaken in the correct manner. In A a goal-kick is the correct award because a goal cannot be scored direct from a place kick, i.e. the kick-off. In C the goalkeeper is penalised for handling the ball outside the area. He should have released it before falling outside the area. 6. A goal kick

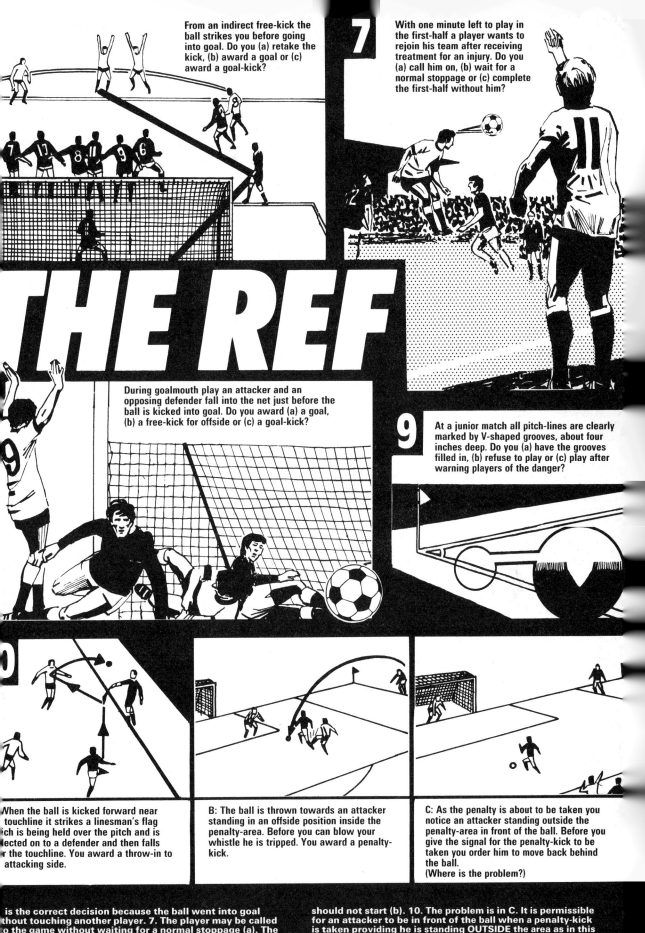

From an indirect free-kick the ball strikes you before going into goal. Do you (a) retake the kick, (b) award a goal or (c) award a goal-kick?

7

With one minute left to play in the first-half a player wants to rejoin his team after receiving treatment for an injury. Do you (a) call him on, (b) wait for a normal stoppage or (c) complete the first-half without him?

THE REF

During goalmouth play an attacker and an opposing defender fall into the net just before the ball is kicked into goal. Do you award (a) a goal, (b) a free-kick for offside or (c) a goal-kick?

9

At a junior match all pitch-lines are clearly marked by V-shaped grooves, about four inches deep. Do you (a) have the grooves filled in, (b) refuse to play or (c) play after warning players of the danger?

When the ball is kicked forward near touchline it strikes a linesman's flag ich is being held over the pitch and is ected on to a defender and then falls the touchline. You award a throw-in to attacking side.

B: The ball is thrown towards an attacker standing in an offside position inside the penalty-area. Before you can blow your whistle he is tripped. You award a penalty-kick.

C: As the penalty is about to be taken you notice an attacker standing outside the penalty-area in front of the ball. Before you give the signal for the penalty-kick to be taken you order him to move back behind the ball.
(Where is the problem?)

is the correct decision because the ball went into goal thout touching another player. 7. The player may be called o the game without waiting for a normal stoppage (a). The e factor is not relevant. 8. A goal should be awarded (a) ovided the attacker is making no attempt to interfere with y or an opponent. 9. If it is possible to have the lines filled but still clear, (a) is the best solution. Otherwise the match should not start (b). 10. The problem is in C. It is permissible for an attacker to be in front of the ball when a penalty-kick is taken providing he is standing OUTSIDE the area as in this situation. In A the action taken is correct. The linesman's flag is considered part of the game's equipment, similar to a goal-post. In B the penalty award is correct. The attacker cannot be offside from a throw-in.

FRANK BLUNSTONE

BE MY GUEST

FRANK BLUNSTONE went into management when his career as a Chelsea and England winger (five caps) was ended by injury in 1964. He became team boss of Brentford, and later No.2 to Tommy Docherty at Manchester United and Derby.

He had started his career with his home town club, Crewe, and in 13 years in the game he played more than 400 matches.

Now he and his wife Doreen run a guest house at Putney, in South-west London.

Says Frank: "I bought this six-bedroom property when I was playing. Now it keeps us ticking over in business.

"We'll never make a fortune at it, but we enjoying looking after the people who come to stay with us, and are happy in what we are doing. I find time for a bit of golf, but the only football I see these days is on the telly."

RON HARRIS

£2 MILLION MAN

RON HARRIS, who captained Chelsea to FA Cup triumph in 1970 and the Cup-Winners' Cup a year later, belongs to that rare breed of ex-footballers who are now millionaires.

Now 45, he sold his house and borrowed from the bank to buy a run-down golf club, Bremhill Park, in Wiltshire, for £300,000. That was five years ago.

With his wife Lee and their two grown-up sons, he worked round the clock to turn it into a super club .... and in January 1990, he sold it for £2m.

"The deal set us up for life," says Ron. The family now live on a farm just outside Swindon and he says: "When I'm not pottering around, I'm often away playing golf, in competitions and charity events."

JOHN PRATT

TOTTENHAM'S EURO KING

JOHN PRATT made almost 500 appearances for Tottenham in a playing career which spanned 15 years at White Hart Lane. He was a UEFA Cup winner in 1972, against Wolves, and won a League Cup winners medal the following season.

Pratt played alongside such greats as Jimmy Greaves, Pat Jennings through to Ossie Ardiles and Glenn Hoddle. He was rewarded with a 23,000 crowd at his 1978 testimonial.

After Tottenham, he played for Portland Trailblazers, in America, before returning to coach the Tottenham youth side in 1983 and eventually became assistant manager to Peter Shreeve.

Pratt failed to find another job in football after Tottenham and now works on his own successful window cleaning round in Chigwell, Essex. He still plays football for his local Essex team.

EY NOW?

ENGLAND'S World Cup-winning manager Sir Alf Ramsey described Martin Peters as being a player 10 years ahead of his time.

Peters, capped 67 times by England and Britain's first £200,000 player in 1970, is now a Sales and Promotional Executive for Motor Plan, a mechanical and breakdown insurance company in Dagenham.

On the 30th July, 1966, Peters was seconds away from becoming 'The Man Who Won England The World Cup'. He scored the goal that put England 2-1 up against West Germany in the Final at Wembley. But eternal fame was snatched from his grasp when Hans Weber equalised for the Germans.

That enabled Peters' West Ham teammate Geoff Hurst to score twice in extra-time and complete the hat-trick which secured England's historic 4-2 win.

"Before I joined Motor Plan, I missed not being involved in football. But now I am too busy to notice," says Peters, who also played for Tottenham and Norwich City.

By coincidence Peters' Hammers and England side-kick Hurst also worked for Motor Plan before joining BAC Windows, who sponsor West Ham.

MARTIN PETERS

DAVID FAIRCLOUGH

CASH COURSE

SALES CHIEF

DAVID FAIRCLOUGH had to move abroad to shake off the 'Supersub' tag he had at Liverpool.

Fairclough found fame in the 1970s as the scorer of vital goals when thrust late into the action. But he failed to establish himself as a permanent fixture and left for Swiss side FC Lucerne in 1982.

Fairclough ended up at Wigan Athletic in 1990 after spells with Oldham, Belgian side Beveren and Tranmere Rovers.

In his 10 years at Anfield, Fairclough won four League titles, two European Cups, two League Cups, one UEFA Cup and four Charity Shield medals. There was also an England B cap.

Fairclough remembers two goals he scored in particular, one in a 'derby' against Everton in 1976 and the goal that beat St Etienne in a 1977 European Cup Quarter-Final tie at Anfield.

"It was a long ball from Ray Kennedy, put where I used to hunt for the ball. I chested it down, shook off the centre-half and went on to score," says Fairclough.

Fairclough is planning for the future. He has taken a journalism course and is learning about the world of financial consultancy.

WHERE were you 25 years ago? If you are over 30 you will almost certainly remember. There has never been a time quite like it for English soccer.

Just a month or two before history was created, the English soccer season was coming to a close. Liverpool were League Champions (who else?). Leeds were second and Burnley – yes Burnley – were third with the same number of points.

In Division Two, Manchester City, Southampton and Coventry filled the top three places. The top two went up, replacing relegated Northampton and Blackburn Rovers. Hull City and Millwall were promoted from Division Three, Queens Park Rangers just missed out.

Everton beat Sheffield Wednesday in the FA Cup Final 3-2, while in the League Cup we saw the last of the two-legged finals, West Brom beating West Ham 5-3 on aggregate.

WHEN ENG
THE W

In Scotland, Celtic were Champions, commencing an amazing run of nine consecutive title wins. They won the Scottish League Cup as well but were stopped from taking the treble when beaten by Rangers 1-0 in the Scottish Cup Final.

Real Madrid were European Cup winners for the sixth time, Borussia Dortmund beat Liverpool 2-1 in Glasgow to win the European Cup-Winners' Cup and Barcelona won the Fairs Cup, the former UEFA Cup.

Bobby Charlton was Footballer of the Year and Jock Stein of Celtic was Manager of the Year. The soccer scene was live and well in Britain and there was a buzz throughout the soccer world about the forthcoming

World Cup tournament in England.

Eleven English footballers were soon to become national heroes. The home of soccer, its rightful birthplace was to be set ablaze by the heroes of 1966.

Alf Ramsey, former Spurs and England international, had performed miracles as manager of Ipswich. By

public demand he became England manager in 1963 following an illustrious 17-year command by Walter Winterbottom.

Ramsey's first game in charge was a heavy 5-2 defeat by France in Paris. Facing a barrage of press questions, he boldly stated that England could

Portugal's Eusebio grounded many defences.

Hurst strikes and England are Cha
of the world.

But everyone was still determined to enjoy the eighth World Cup.

At last the teams flew in, among them the superstars of Italy, West Germany, Brazil, Russia, Portugal, Argentina, Uruguay and others. Pele, Eusebio, Beckenbauer, Yashin – they were all there alongside the unlikely lads of North Korea who won the hearts of the people just as the Cameroon did in 1990.

After the opening ceremony, England took the Wembley stage against Uruguay. It was a disappointing 0-0 draw. England's attack was blunted by the Uruguayan defensive screen.

The next match looked like going the same way with Mexico happy to emulate their Latin-American cousins. But England had the force with them. The force was in the shape of Bobby Charlton's right foot. A run, a look and a scorching shot from 40 yards or more. The ball flew into the net. There was a stunned silence and then Wembley erupted. England were on their way.

AND RULED ORLD

A FASCINATING LOOK BACK TO JULY 1966 AND THE GREATEST DAY IN ENGLAND'S SOCCER HISTORY…

win the World Cup. By the time those words reached the daily sports pages the whole country read the message, – ' "We'll win the World Cup", says Alf.'

The results leading up to the tournament were not confidence-inspiring. A 3-2 home defeat by Austria brought forth some derision.

France were next. It was not a brilliant match, but a goal in each half from Roger Hunt ensured England's passage into the Quarter-Finals. Some of the disbelievers fell silent. England were beginning to play some attractive football. Argentina did their best to change all that.

Their only real contribution to the game was walking on to the pitch. They kicked everything but the ball and only that after a free-kick had been given against them. The ultimate disgrace was the sending-off of their ill-tempered captain Antonio Rattin and their manhandling of the unfortunate referee. The ultimate response was a goal from Geoff Hurst, who had been drafted in to replace the injured Jimmy Greaves.

Portugal became the first team to put a goal past England when Eusebio scored from a penalty in their Semi-Final encounter. But it was more of a late consolation since England were already two goals to the good, Bobby Charlton having scored one in each half.

Suddenly the country realised that England were in the Final of the World Cup. West Germany were the opposition. The date was Saturday 30th July. The England line-up was the same as for the previous two matches:-

Gordon Banks (Leicester); George Cohen (Fulham), Ray Wilson (Everton), Nobby Stiles (Manchester United), Jack Charlton (Leeds), Bobby Moore (West Ham); Alan Ball (Everton), Roger Hunt (Liverpool), Bobby Charlton (Manchester United), Geoff Hurst (West Ham), Martin Peters (West Ham).

West Germany took the lead following a defensive mistake. The home fans were temporarily stunned. England fought back. Skipper Bobby Moore was fouled, took the free-kick himself and found the head of fellow Hammer Hurst. The score was 1-1.

In the second-half Martin Peters got the whole of England celebrating, but a late free-kick led to the Germans equalising.

Extra-time needed and Ramsey rallied his troops. Then Geoff Hurst created his own piece of soccer history. He broke the deadlock with a goal that was hotly disputed by the Germans, but allowed by the officials. Then with the fans whistling for full-time, he sealed it.

In the dying seconds Hurst somehow found the energy to break loose, run a full 70 yards and hammer home a fierce left-foot shot that put the matter beyond all doubt. England had won the World Cup!

CONTINUED OVERLEAF

WHEN ENGLAND RULED THE WORLD

Germany equalise in the last seconds but England were not to be denied their greatest triumph.

Here we are 25 years later knowing that a year ago in Italy, England were good enough to do it again. Three years from now we hope to be off to the United States to perhaps repeat history. But what of those 12 heroes of '66. Where are they now?

GORDON BANKS was forced into early retirement after a car crash. He played for Stoke after Leicester but his career ended in 1972. Today Gordon still lives near Leicester. He runs his own successful corporate entertainment company organising special events and functions for businesses. He also still coaches some Division One goalkeepers and pops up from time to time on TV and radio to comment on matches.

GEORGE COHEN only completed another two seasons. In a 1968-69 League match at Craven Cottage he sustained a serious knee injury and despite several operations and attempted comebacks he was forced to retire. George tried his hand at non-League management but there was a bigger battle to come since he had a fierce fight with cancer. Happily he won and was able to continue his life in Kent where he is a property developer.

Perhaps the most bizarre change of career was that of RAY WILSON. Injuries also brought his career to a close perhaps a little earlier than he would have liked. Ray moved out of football and into the funeral business and that is what he is still doing today.

NOBBY STILES, England's impish half-back continued his success story with Manchester United, like Bobby Charlton, adding a European Cup medal to his collection of honours. After hanging up his boots, Nobby tried his hand at management but while his coaching skills were evident, Nobby did not seem to sit comfortably in the manager's chair.

He is still coaching though and is as committed as ever to soccer and as fervent as ever in his following of Manchester United.

JACK CHARLTON seems to have quietly faded into oblivion doesn't he! Big Jack is probably even bigger in soccer now than he was as a player. In Ireland they believe he can walk on water. When Jack's career ended he started two new ones. In soccer management he worked wonders for Sheffield Wednesday, Middlesbrough and Newcastle and then performed miracles for the Republic of Ireland. His other career has seen him host TV programmes about field sports like fishing and shooting. Never a dull moment for Jack.

BOBBY MOORE, the captain, went on to collect a total of 108 full England caps. He also masterminded one of the finest spells in the history of West Ham United. Bobby also tried his hand at management but it did not work. Instead he entered the world of sports journalism and also made a number of TV and film appearances including a major part in the famous 'Escape to Victory' movie with Michael Caine and Sylvester Stallone.

ALAN BALL played his last England game in 1975. Since ending his playing career he has been as involved in the game as ever, managing several clubs, his most successful period being with Portsmouth whom he took from Division Three to Division One.

When ROGER HUNT moved out of football he moved out completely. He still enjoys watching games of course but did not want to go through the trials of soccer management. Instead he joined his brother in a family transport and haulage business which is still going strong in Lancashire.

BOBBY CHARLTON is still deeply involved in the game. He is a greatly respected voice of soccer. Bobby did not enjoy his time in soccer management but his football schools, television appearances and place at the Manchester United boardroom table have kept him as prominent and popular as ever, particularly abroad where he is in great demand to appear on countless TV shows and at special events.

GEOFF HURST continued his career into the 1970s before trying his hand, largely unsuccessfully, at management. He is still remembered as the man who scored a hat-trick in the World Cup Final and is still called upon for personal appearances and endorsements. Worked in insurance before switching to a window company.

MARTIN PETERS has had an almost identical career to that of his mate Geoff Hurst. He also went into motor insurance after a less than satisfactory soccer management spell at Sheffield United. Martin had played for Spurs and Norwich after his Upton Park days.

ALF RAMSEY became Sir Alf. He continued as England boss until 1974. Failure, albeit narrow failure, to win the World Cup again seemed to upset the hierarchy of the Football Association and Sir Alf was no longer welcome at Lancaster Gate. He and the England fans were less than pleased. Ramsey withdrew from public life into his home at Ipswich. Only recently has he started to be seen around again and there is a happy ending in that he is now a part of Graham Taylor's England 'think tank'.

And that is how we find them all today, 25 years later. Still with the timeless sound ringing in their ears, echoing through the years –
"England – England – England!"

CHARNLEY – SCOTLAND'S GAZZA

John Lambie.

PAUL GASCOIGNE is not unique in British football; in CHIC CHARNLEY, the 28-year-old Partick Thistle midfielder, Scotland has had someone in the Court Jester mould for some time.

In fact, there are times when Charnley, previously with St Mirren, Ayr, Pollock Juniors, Clydebank and Hamilton, has made Gascoigne seem positively inhibited and conservative.

The examples of his attempts to add some fun to the game are numerous.

One of the most outrageous was when he sold a dummy to an opponent and then allowed the ball to run out of play as he bowed theatrically to the crowd.

Even his former Hamilton and Partick manager, John Lambie, one of the game's hard men, laughs when recalling a team talk in which he used a tea set to illustrate the tactical faults which had caused his Hamilton team to lose 8-0 to Celtic. "Hey gaffer," Charnley shouted. "Is this a Cup-tie?"

Lambie insists that the game could do with more characters like Charnley and Gascoigne. In Chic's case, however, the saddest part of his ability to bring enjoyment to the fans is that he has reaped such little reward for it.

He has extraordinary vision and technical skills, like Gascoigne, he can create goals out of nothing. But, unlike Gazza, he has allowed himself to become more of a cult figure than an outstanding footballer.

He admits that, on becoming a full-time professional with St Mirren, at 19, he was unable to adjust to the strict discipline imposed by their manager, Alex Miller. He then spent more than two years out of the game, preferring to spend his Saturday's watching his beloved Celtic.

It says much about the self-destructive side of his nature that Clydebank, who brought him back in to the league in 1987, and who have always prided themselves on making a profit on such skilful players in the transfer market, let him go for nothing.

However, many feel that it is still not too late for him to reach the top. His outrageous skills have attracted the attention of a number of big clubs and, in the past, even Celtic have toyed with the idea of taking a chance on him.

All his family are avid Celtic fans, and he says: "My late grandmother wanted me to become a top-class professional footballer much more than I did. If she thought there was a wee chance of me signing for Celtic, she would probably come back."

HOWARD

Leeds United are back in the big time where, according to their fervent followers at least, they belong. And what's more, they intend to stay there.

Having just completed their first season back in Division One for eight years, the Elland Road club is building for the future determined to avoid another depressing fall from grace and power.

And, although Howard Wilkinson's class of '91 might still be a few diplomas short of Don Revie's stylish students of the 70s, they may not be too far away from graduation day.

For the majority of last season they took the top flight by storm and served notice of their intentions as early as the opening day when,

inspired by Gordon Strachan, they stormed into a 3-0 first-half lead at Everton.

They eventually ran out 3-2 winners in that game, a performance which was to mirror their overall achievements during a season when they threatened to deliver only to flatter to deceive.

Their title challenge, which appeared to be gathering momentum when they reached third place in December, fizzled out early in the new year as the competition turned into a two-horse race.

In national hunt terms they started well, but hit a few fences half way round and faded on the run-in. Sure to do better next time out.

United's fortunes in the two major Cup competitions took a similar turn for the worse when they looked set to go the distance.

Leeds bowed out to Manchester United in the Rumblelows Cup last term.

FOR THE RECORD

GROUND: Elland Road Capacity: 40,176
RECORD attendance: 57,892 v Sunderland, 1967
PRESIDENT: Rt Hon.The Earl of Harewood
CHAIRMAN: L. Silver
MANAGER: Howard Wilkinson
YEAR formed: 1919 (turned pro 1920)
NICKNAME: United/Whites
COLOURS: All white (change:all yellow)
RECORD League victory: 8-0 v Leicester (Division One) 1934
RECORD Cup victory: 10-0 v Lynn Oslo (European Cup) 1969
RECORD defeat: 1-8 v Stoke (Division One) 1934
MOST League points (2 for a win): 67 (Division One) 1968-69
MOST League points (3 for a win): 85 (Division Two) 1989-90
MOST League goals: 98 (Division Two) 1927-28
HIGHEST League scorer (season): John Charles (1953-54) 42
HIGHEST League scorer (total): Peter Lorimer (1965-86) 168
MOST capped player: Billy Bremner (Scotland) 54
MOST League appearances: Jack Charlton (1953-73) 629

Arsenal ended Gordon Strachan's interest in the FA Cup after a titanic struggle.

WAY!

It was goals all the way for Lee Chapman last season.

In the Rumbelows Cup they were forced to bow to the superior sudden-death knowledge of past masters Manchester United at the Semi-Final hurdle, while in the FA Cup they ran out of steam against Arsenal after a titanic four-match struggle.

But, having re-built a side capable of challenging for honours, the signs look good for Howard Wilkinson.

The fight of Mel Sterland and David Batty; the flair of Gary McAllister and Gordon Strachan; and the finishing of Lee Chapman should stand Leeds in good stead for a while yet.

Whether they can reach the heady heights the mighty Leeds side of the late 1960s aspired to remains to be seen.

The most important thing is that the club has finally emerged from a spell in the doldrums which tainted the all-conquering image built up during the Revie era.

Up until the mid-1960s, however, the club had failed to win a single major trophy. Second Division Champions in 1924 was their only real claim to fame. Revie soon changed that.

All their League and Cup triumphs – at home and abroad – came in a glorious six-year spell between 1968 and 1974.

During that time Leeds won the League Championship twice; the European Fairs Cup twice, the FA Cup and the League Cup once. They were also runners-up in the League three times; the European Cup, the Cup-Winners' Cup and the FA Cup (twice).

The list of honours makes impressive reading, but it also presents a daunting task for Wilkinson as he prepares to restore former glories to the once proud club.

Billy Bremner holds aloft the 1972 FA Cup.

STAR CROSSWORD

ACROSS

1 Scottish club Airdrie play on this park (10)
8 Partick or Meadowbank perhaps (4)
9 You might find this little horror at Old Trafford (3,5)
10 Animals found at Boothferry Park (6)
11 ...... s – 'keeper at The Dell (6)
12 Trevor Brooking wore this number with pride for West Ham (3)
13 Crosby ... but not Bing (4)
15 Old Trafford ace formerly with the Hammers (4)
17 A League footballer ... in short (3)
19 You might elope to join this non-League club (6)
21 Liverpool-born Everton striker (6)
23 Former Dutch international famed for his powerful shooting from long range (4,4)
24 An ex-boss or an aid to referees (4)
25 The men from Turf Moor are also known as this (3,7)

DOWN

2 They play at Elm Park (7)
3 Newcastle boss or former Chelsea idol (5)
4 League Champions in 1978 and European Cup winners in 1979 (6)
5 Barry – 60s and 70s striker whose seven clubs included Watford and Blackburn (6)
6 Top German club Dynamo – come from here (7)
7 Balding full-back or a transfer fee (5)
14 What defenders have to do under attack (7)
16 English defender who had a spell in Italy (7)
17 FA Cup finalists in 1990 (6)
18 Scoreline in the replay of the above game (3,3)
20 FA Cup replay, perhaps (5)
22 West German scorer in the 1966 World Cup Final (5)

(Crossword grid, partially filled in by hand:)

- 1 Across: BROOMFIELD
- 8 Across: JAGS
- 9 Across: RED DEVIL(S)
- 10 Across: TIGERS
- 11 Across: ANDREW
- 12 Across: TEN
- 13 Across: GARY
- 15 Across: INCE
- 17 Across: PRO
- 19 Across: GRETNA
- 21 Across: NEWELL
- 23 Across: ARIE HAAN
- 25 Across: THE CLARETS

One of these clubs is linked to 17 Down.

ANSWERS ON PAGE 121

See 23 Across.

HISTORY looms large at Highbury and the responsibility of wearing the No.9 shirt generates a unique pressure. In fact, it can be murder.

After Frank Stapleton left North London for Old Trafford in 1981, a void was created at the heart of the Arsenal attack which a procession of strikers were unable to fill.

John Hawley, Ray Hankin, the young Lee Chapman, Raphael Meade, an ageing Paul Mariner and Charlie Nicholas all tried and failed to live up to the heights demanded of an Arsenal centre-forward.

Yet today, Gunners appear to have solved their striking problem and the shirt of the fabled Ted Drake who scored 43 goals in one season for the club in 1934-5, is today worn with cool assurance and quiet confidence by Alan Smith.

But Smith admits that when he first joined the club from Leicester City in 1987 he was surprised to find how little time he was given to settle in by the media.

"We started badly that season," Smith reflects, "I was partnering Charlie Nicholas up front and we failed to win our first three games and what's more we were beaten in two of them.

Alan Smith rates Leeds defender Chris Whyte as one of his toughest opponents.

DIAL 9 FOR MURDER

THE ALAN SMITH STORY

"I was immediately put under pressure and because I didn't score in any of those games there was some harping on about whether or not I was the right man for the job in the press. – I felt my Arsenal career was in danger!"

For the fourth game of that 1987 season, against Portsmouth at Highbury, George Graham dropped Charlie Nicholas and Smith was partnered in attack by an enthusiastic Perry Groves.

Smith continues the story: "It was a warm late summer day, the crowd was behind us and for some reason we relaxed. We played some good football, ran out 6-0 winners, and I scored a hat-trick."

Those three vital goals immediately won over the demanding Arsenal fans, Smith relaxed, and he has worn that No.9 shirt ever since.

He was a crucial member of the championship winning side of 1988-9, finishing top scorer in the First Division with 23 goals, which won him the Adidas/Shoot Golden Shoe Award.

Apart from his own form what has pleased Alan most over the last year?

"The arrival of Anders Limpar," he says. "He is such an exciting player. His dribbling skills and ability to score unexpected goals has added a new dimension to our game. As soon as he arrived we created plenty of chances again."

Like Limpar, Smith believes there's more to his game than just goal scoring. He spends much of each game with his back to goal bringing others into the game, by shielding the ball and laying it off.

It is this part of his game which is rarely highlighted but which is crucial to the success of George Graham's game-plan.

Also Smith is a consistently selfless player, he has good control and skill for a big man and surprisingly for a striker he shares with Gary Lineker, his old Leicester striking partner, the admirable record of never being booked

"I get quite a bit of stick about this at the club from the players who think it strange that a big centre-forward has never been booked. But I don't make many tackles do I?" he jokes.

"But seriously I am fairly placid and even-tempered and never retaliate, even though playing with my back to goal means that I receive my fair share of knocks and kicks from defenders.

"Gary Lineker has a mild temperament and is very laid back; but never being booked is not something I'm conscious of when I am involved in a game."

Born in Birmingham in 1962, Smith began his professional career with Leicester City, when Jock Wallace signed him from non-League Alvechurch when he was 19.

He was at polytechnic studying modern languages at the time, having left school with ten 0 levels and three A levels.

He went on to play more than 200 games in all competitions for Leicester City, scoring 84 goals, and he recalls that the Midlands club won promotion in his first season.

A hat-trick against Portsmouth early in the 1987-88 season quickly won over the demanding Highbury fans.

Alan's goalscoring form for non-League Alvechurch persuaded Leicester City to sign him.

"When we got into the First Division we struggled, we had one or two good results, but it was a battle. I did learn a lot though. I played alongside Gary Lineker for a time, and our manager Gordon Milne was a good influence on me."

With Peter Beardsley out of favour with Graham Taylor, Steve Bull lacking the close control required of an international forward and with the jury still out on the explosive Ian Wright, the search for a suitable foil for Lineker goes on.

So after playing with Gary at Leicester does Smith think that he can be as successful with Lineker at England level as they were at City?

"I'm frequently asked this question," he admits, "and what I will say is that I was pleased to partner Gary against Turkey last year.

"I enjoyed playing with Gary in the past, we complemented each other because our style of play differs – whereas I like to participate in the build-up, Gary is very direct and runs onto through balls."

Smith will say no more except that

he enjoys being involved in the England set-up and "that it is up to Graham Taylor."

But even if he never teams up with Lineker again, in his career at Highbury, the likeable Smith has had his fair share of partners.

He is an admirer of the "great ball skills" of the maverick Charlie Nicholas and he believes that Paul Merson has terrific talent.

"He's very exciting, has pace, is versatile and can play through the centre and on the right flank. He flits between defenders using his speed and he is strong running with the ball," says Smith.

The tall Arsenal striker is also not surprised that Niall Quinn, who served as his deputy for so long at Highbury, has settled in so effectively at Manchester City.

"At Arsenal he led the line in George Graham's first season. He was inexperienced then and under a lot of pressure. For a big man he has good ball skills, but we could always see that in training. Although we were not the perfect striking

Paul Merson.

partnership, the few times we played together we did quite well."

Capped by England, Smith has played against some top class central defenders, but who does he rate domestically?

"The Leeds pair, Chris Whyte and Chris Fairclough, give you a hard game because they mark you very tightly," he confides.

Now 29, Smith, who cites his dad Bob as a particularly strong influence on his football development, could have joined Chelsea and possibly Manchester United in 1987, but says that he has "no regrets" about joining Arsenal.

Alan still has a year left on his contract and will continue to play for the club as long as he is wanted.

"I have no plans to move elsewhere. Since playing for Arsenal I have developed an affinity with the place which I know will never leave me. I suspect I will follow them into retirement."

As Arsenal defend the League Championship their No. 9 shirt could not be in better hands.

HAT-TRICK

John Barnes scores the second of his three goals against Coventry in May 1990.

Steve Bull – a hat-trick hero for Wolves.

The definition of a hat-trick has changed since football first began.

Everybody knows that a hat-trick is three goals in the same game, but did you know that in the old days those goals had to be scored consecutively?

If that were the case nowadays, there would be considerably fewer hat-tricks scored.

So just who are the hat-trick aces? Well, not surprisingly, Liverpool are way out in front.

Not only have they been the outstanding team of the past decade but they have also had the top goalscorers like Ian Rush, Kenny Dalglish and John Aldridge.

Rush was the last player to score five goals in a First Division match, although Arsenal's Tony Woodcock also achieved that feat on the same day, October 29, 1983.

Rush smashed five past Luton as they were hammered 6-0 at Anfield, while Woodcock scored five of Arsenal's goals in a 6-2 win over Aston Villa at Villa Park.

One or two individual hat-trick records seem unlikely ever to be broken.

Jimmy Greaves managed six hat-tricks for Chelsea in 1960-61, while the legendary Dixie Dean retired with 37 trebles to his credit.

In the last decade, however, a couple of hat-trick feats did enter the record books.

Alan Shearer's hat-trick for Southampton against Arsenal in April 1988 made him the youngest player to achieve this feat, beating the record set by a young Greavsie some 30 years earlier, by a few weeks.

In season 1987-88, Manchester City

ACES

So which teams scored the most hat-tricks?

NB: Only clubs who have completed at least 8 of the last 10 seasons in the Football League are included in this list.

Pos.	Hat-tricks	
1	21	Liverpool
2=	14	Northampton, Wigan
4=	13	Aldershot, Luton
6=	11	Burnley, Southampton, Spurs
9=	10	Chelsea, Colchester, Lincoln, Mansfield, Sheff Utd
14=	9	Bristol C., Cambridge, Ipswich, Nottm F., Portsmouth, Port Vale, Rotherham, Swindon, Wolves
23=	8	Blackburn, Blackpool, Bradford, Everton, Exeter, Huddersfield, Leeds, Millwall, Newcastle, Oldham, Oxford, QPR, Scunthorpe, Sunderland, West Ham, Wimbledon
39=	7	Barnsley, Bolton, Bournemouth, Bury, Carlisle, Chester, Coventry, Gillingham, Leicester, Notts Co, Reading, Stockport, WBA, Wrexham
53=	6	Arsenal, Darlington, Grimsby, Halifax, Hull, L. Orient, Man City, Middlesbrough, Southend, Stoke
63=	5	Chesterfield, Crewe, C. Palace, Man Utd, Newport, Plymouth, Preston, Walsall, Watford, York
73=	4	Derby, Doncaster, Fulham, Hartlepool, Norwich, Peterborough, Swansea, Tranmere
81=	3	Brentford, Brighton, Bristol R., Charlton, Hereford, Sheff Wed, Torquay
88=	2	Aston Villa, Birmingham, Rochdale
91	1	Cardiff

came only the third club this ntury to have three hat-tricks in e game. During their 10-1 molition of Huddersfield, Tony dcock, Paul Stewart and David hite – all scored trebles. Wonder ho kept the match ball?

Wolves provide one of the most credible hat-trick tales.

From season 1980-81 until late in e 1986-87 season, the men from olineux had failed to register a ngle hat-trick. But since then they ve scored nine.

The reason is simple: Steve Bull. lly has scored all nine of their cent hat-tricks and if anyone is to allenge the records of Greaves and an, it's seems likely to be him.

Without doubt, the worst record ring the past ten years belongs to rdiff City. The last person to score hat-trick for them was Gary evens in a 5-4 win over Cambridge n March 1982!

Jimmy Greaves.

Paul Stewart.

David White.

PLAY FOOTBALL...
THE GAZZA WAY

Exercises and warm-up

Even if it's not match day and you're just training you shouldn't even think of starting until you've done some simple exercises.

Start off with a mild jog, shaking the body as you go along, then checking and going the opposite way. Change the pace to little bursts of running, kicking up your heels to touch your hands which you hold behind you.

Don't start stretching until you're fully warmed up.

Run with your knees up with a bit of high kicking, patting our knees as you run. Jog with your arms up and down in the air, thinking of the tune 'Let's all have a disco'.

Now start stretching. First the neck, then the arms, a bit of hip sway (like a hula-hoop expert) and then start on the legs. Buy the book and you'll see how I work the groin, thighs, hamstrings, ankles and calves.

Each person will develop their own warm-up routine. However you do it, it's important to realise how much work you should do before a game to fulfill your potential during a match.

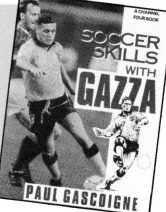

Taken from the book SOCCER SKILLS WITH GAZZA by Paul Gascoigne and Mel Stein, published by Stanley Paul. Price: £6.99.

A CHANNEL FOUR BOOK

SOCCER SKILLS WITH GAZZA

PAUL GASCOIGNE

Control

Don't stamp on the ball (above). Trap the ball with the sole of the boot like I'm doing here.

I've always wanted to be a traffic policeman!

As with everything else in life – even driving a car – if you are out of control you take risks. When you are in control, you feel good.

I've set up a number of exercises in the book to illustrate how you can improve your control and make you a better player. You can use cones, garden gnomes, deck chairs, spades ... anything will do. Practice is the key.

Practice the basics of trapping the ball, both when standing still and running.

You can use the sole of your boot, but make sure your foot is at an angle. Don't stamp on the ball! Collecting the ball on the instep and cushioning it on the thigh are two other options.

Kicking

The first rule of kicking is don't use the toe of the boot. I might use the toe for a lob or a chip on the goalie but apart from that it's always the inside or outside of the foot – or the heel if I feel particularly cheeky.

As with almost everything else in the game, kicking is a question of touch and feel. If you're going to go anywhere in the sport you have to have a naturally good kicking technique.

Kick the ball with the full instep.

And it is important that, whenever you practice, use both feet. Always work on your weaker leg.

Also practice kicking with both the inside and outside of the foot. Both have a part to play.

Practice techniques with your friends by splitting into two lines on either side of the goal to vary the angle of the ball coming in.

Have somebody on each side throwing the ball in for you to trap and kick. At this stage don't worry about power, concentrate on accuracy.

Here's the perfect example of a standing defensive power header.

Passing and vision

Football is a team game. Sometimes you have to decide to go it alone, sometimes to pass. It's a split second decision.

On occasions I've been accused of being greedy, but I don't agree and I wouldn't encourage anyone else to be.

You need to be aware of what's going on around you, and to have movement off the ball. If you're standing still you are easy to mark.

It's not difficult to hit a straight ball across the park in your own half. It gets you nowhere. If you are going for a long pass you should be aiming to split a defence with one of your team-mates running on to it. Try and apply backspin with your instep.

There are all types of passes; the side foot along the ground, the back heel pass, the pass down the line with the inside OR outside of the boot. It's all about weighing up the right option for the situation.

Heading

Rule One: keep your eye on the ball. Always resist the temptation to close your eyes and hope for the best.

For the most part it's the forehead you use to head the ball, no other part of the head, and you have to feel confident about it. The only time you use the top of your head is for flick ons.

You have to relax when you're heading. If you are tense with your eyes closed then the head dips and your shoulders are hunched.

Heading is also a question of balance. You have to be able to jump properly and land well balanced.

A good defensive header can turn defence into attack. Get your arms up to give yourself height and velocity, use the whole of the top half of the body. It's almost a swimming motion as you stretch for the ball, flicking your neck at just the right moment. It's balance, power and timing.

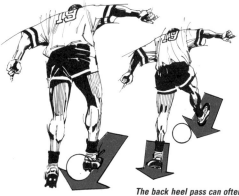

The back heel pass can often surprise your opponent.

End of Part One. More Gazza tips on page 110.

71

Big Jackie Charlton is the giraffe-like Geordie who has made the footballing folk of Ireland walk tall. In world terms the Irish were mere leprechauns until Jack grabbed them by the scruff of the neck and turned them into one of the toughest teams to beat. Just ask England.

JACK'S G

When in Rome ... it's handy to seek a spot of devine intervention – particularly when you are about to face Italy in the World Cup!

A rare moment for Ireland watchers ... it's a goal going in at the wrong end as Ian Rush strikes for Wales in Jack's first game in charge. The Irish got their revenge when the nations last met, though, with a 3-0 win in Wrexham.

ANTS

The moment Irish fans will savour for many years to come – Ray Houghton's Euro goal against England in the 1988 European Championship.

Yet another stalemate against Big Jack's homeland – this time courtesy of Niall Quinn at Wembley.

He's in there somewhere. David O'Leary is mobbed after hitting the penalty that got the Irish to the World Cup Quarter Finals in 1990.

In a 13-year career with Chelsea, AC Milan, Tottenham, West Ham and England, Jimmy Greaves scored more than 400 goals. He was the deadliest striker of his era. So few are more qualified to reveal the game's hard men ... defenders who took no prisoners...

GREAVSIE NAMES FOOTBALL'S TOUGHEST ME

Every time I see Stuart Pearce thundering into a tackle for Nottingham Forest or England, it takes me back 20 years.

Psycho is one of the few genuine 'hard men' left in the British game. He works on the Norman Hunter principle that he'll never get sent-off in the first five minutes so makes sure his first challenge is a real belter.

I've never seen Pearce bottle out of a challenge and it's not very often that an opposing winger comes back for more after a taste of his particular brand of medicine.

But there's not too many others in today's game who I'd call genuinely 'hard'. Bryan Robson and Mark Hughes both like to get stuck in for Manchester United and the lad David Batty puts himself about a bit for Leeds.

People are always comparing Batty to former Leeds skipper Billy Bremner, but in Don Revie's team all 11 were capable of giving a good whack. Norman Hunter was probably the toughest of the lot, but little Johnny Giles wasn't far behind him.

Yet even that Leeds team were a bunch of fairies compared to the defence which Bolton Wanderers used to field when I started in the game for Chelsea in the 1950s.

Even now, 35 years on, the names of that 'Savage Six' are still imprinted firmly in my memory: Eddie Hopkinson (goalie), Roy Hartle and Tommy Banks (full-backs), John Higgins and Bryan Edwards (centre-halfs) and Derek Henning (wing half).

Those guys were undoubtedly the meanest, toughest men to ever pull on a pair of football boots. Every one of them was seven feet wide and no matter what the weather (and let's be honest, it's always raining and freezing cold in Bolton), they always wore short sleeves. What they'd make of John Barnes, in his tights and woolly gloves, doesn't bear thinking about.

Another player today's football fan won't remember is Ray Barlow of West Brom, but when you went in for a tackle with him you'd shake from head to toe.

Then there was Eddie Clamp, Jimmy Scoular and Stan Crowther.

I was absolutely delighted when Chelsea signed Crowther from Manchester United in 1958 because it meant I wouldn't have to play against him any more.

Stan's successor at Stamford Bridge was the one and only Ron Harris and I hated playing him more than anyone else throughout my career.

He wouldn't leave you alone for one second. If you went to the loo at half-time, he'd come with you. You couldn't shake him off until the final whistle, and when he hit you with a challenge it was like being run over by a tank.

But 'Chopper' wasn't just a hatchet man. He was a also a very good, disciplined defender.

The same goes for Liverpool's Tommy Smith, who hated all Southerners and would leather you every opportunity he got. Defenders were allowed to tackle from behind in those days and he never passed up the chance to deck you.

The greatest

Neither did Dave Mackay. Perhaps the greatest player ever to wear a Spurs shirt.

As you can imagine, I took quite a lot of stick from opposing defenders during my career at White Hart Lane. But with Dave behind me and big Bobby Smith alongside me in attack, nobody took any liberties.

Sadly, players like Smithy are a thing of the past. He wouldn't last five minutes in today's game, where you concede a free-kick for breathing on a goalie and get sent-off for challenging a forward 50 yards from goal.

Today's game doesn't lend itself to tough nuts and it's unfair to make

...ave Mac... was my m... with Spurs. With him around nobody took liberties.

Bolton's 'Savage Six' ... Roy Hartle, Derek Henning, Eddie Hopkinson, John Higgins, Bryan Edwards and Tom Banks.

AN MACHINE

comparisons with those men of 20 years ago because they are a totally different breed.

Today's player is quicker, fitter and probably a stone and a half lighter. Defenders in the 50s and 60s had to be bulky because the ball was like a rock, the boots were bigger and harder and, more often than not, you'd be ploughing your way through three feet of mud.

So how did I manage to survive for so long against such cavemen?

Balance and the ability to roll out of a challenge had a lot to do it, but the ability to take a bloody good whack and not let it show also had a lot to do with it.

It makes me cringe when I watch the World Cup and see players like Klinsmann, Maradona and Schillaci rolling over in agony when they've hardly been touched.

I wouldn't have dreamed of doing that because the biggest sin a striker could commit was letting an opponent know that he'd hurt you.

We developed an ability to carry a bit of pain which is missing from today's game.

When I look at the modern physio's medical bag it makes me chuckle. They've got bottles, sprays, ice packs, bandages and enough supplies to keep a pharmacist happy for a month.

At Spurs in the 60s we had dear old Cecil Pointon with a sponge and a bucket of cold water. It didn't matter which part of your anatomy was injured, he'd slap his freezing cold sponge right on your privates. The shock was so great you'd forget all about any other injuries!

Liverpool iron-man Tommy Smith hated all Southerners

'Psycho' Pearce stands no nonsense, even if your name is Paul Gascoigne.

1 Stuart Ian Slater was born in Sudbury, Suffolk, on 27th March, 1969 and attended Sudbury Upper School.

2 He was a keen Ipswich Town fan as a boy – his favourite players were Portman Road Dutch internationals Arnold Muhren and Frans Thijssen, and amongst his most treasured possessions are the autographs of Ipswich's FA Cup and UEFA Cup winning teams.

3 Stuart was not a great student and left school without getting any qualifications.

4 If he hadn't become a footballer, Stuart would probably have ended up working for his father's building firm.

5 Both Arsenal and Ipswich showed an interest in Slater. He trained with Ipswich for three years, but West Ham managed to lure the youngster away before he could sign on with the Suffolk club as an apprentice. West Ham manager at the time was John Lyall, now boss at Second Division Ipswich.

6 West Ham became interested after watching him play for Essex team Langham Lions, where Stuart had been top scorer for three seasons.

7 West Ham signed Stuart after he left school at 16 – and was immediately put on a diet of hamburgers, steaks and chocolate because he needed to put on some weight.

8 He managed to put on an extra two and a half stone – and his height shot up nine inches. His weight is now stabilised at about 10st 4lb.

9 Stuart made his full League debut for The Hammers on 3rd October, 1987 when West Ham drew 1-1 with Derby County.

10 He made 18 League appearances during the 1988-89 season before the East London club were relegated to Division Two - since then he has commanded a regular place in West Ham's first team. After one scintillating performance a leading manager described Stuart as "another Eusebio".

STUART SLATER

14 He is house-hunting at the moment; but in the meantime he is living with his grandparents in Chelmsford, Essex, during the week. He goes back home to his parents' house in Sudbury during weekends.

15 Stuart is not married and he doesn't have a regular girlfriend – but he says that his ideal woman would have to be easy going.

16 The young West Ham forward drives a sponsored Sierra but his team-mates don't think much of his ability behind the wheel: "They think I'm a lousy driver," he says.

17 Stuart is a whizz-kid at juggling the ball. His record stands at 11,000. "I only stopped because my neck and back were hurting." He is set to challenge world record holder Rob Walters, cousin of Rangers star Mark, in a charity juggling event. "I'll do my best but Rob has done 67,000," says Slater.

18 Stuart is a keep-fit fanatic who can often be found in the weight-training room after club training sessions.

19 Slater has not had many serious injuries in his short career but he can't play on hard frosty pitches without wearing a special instep in his boot to keep a damaged Achilles tendon at bay.

12 His worst time came after Oldham's 6-0 defeat of West Ham in the 1989-90 Littlewoods Cup Semi-Final first-leg – he felt so bad he didn't want to go out for weeks afterwards.

11 Stuart's most embarrassing incident took place at Sunderland during the 1989-90 season when he missed an open goal: "The ball came across to me and I just screwed it wide of the post. Luckily I'd scored quite a good goal just before that."

13 Stuart thinks that Forest's Des Walker has been the most difficult opponent he's come up against so far, although his own West Ham team-mate Julian Dicks comes a close second in training.

20 His fierce tackling has earned him the nickname Chopper from his team-mates, but he claims his goalscoring and heading skills need improving.

GREAT GUN

TED DRAKE
182 games 136 goals

CENTRE-FORWARD who set a Football League record in 1935 which might never be broken. He scored all of Arsenal's SEVEN goals in their thrashing of Aston Villa at Villa Park, and later claimed it should have been eight.

The one that got away hit the underside of the crossbar and, Drake insists, dropped over the line and out again. But the referee waved play on and told Drake not be greedy.

Drake had joined The Gunners from Southampton for £6,000 a year before that amazing day and in his first season scored 42 goals, which is still a club record. He was The Gunners' top scorer in the five seasons before the Second World War, helping the club to two League titles and an FA Cup triumph.

LIAM BRADY
306 games 59 goals

IRISHMAN known as Chippy from his earliest days at Highbury because he ate chips with everything. But right from his League debut in 1973, when he began the move that brought the only goal in a 1-0 victory over Birmingham, his nickname had an altogether different definition with his adoring Arsenal fans.

Brady's left foot was exquisite – a precision instrument that unlocked defences to such effect that Arsenal reached four Cup Finals in three years with him in their side. His greatest hour came in the 1979 FA Cup Final, when he created two of the goals in Arsenal's thrilling 3-2 triumph over Manchester United.

There was disappointment in his final season, when Arsenal were defeated in both the FA Cup and Cup-Winners' Cup finals. But the biggest blow of all, to Arsenal's fans, was when Brady agreed to a £600,000 transfer to Juventus in July 1981.

ALEX JAMES
259 games 27 goals

ARSENAL'S oldest fans would probably describe Paul Gascoigne as a poor man's Alex James because Wee Alex was the most dazzling darling of them all. His sublime skill was only matched by his wicked

sense of humour. His trademark were the long baggy shorts he wore, he said, to keep his knees warm.

Herbert Chapman, the greatest Arsenal manager of them all, beat Liverpool, Manchester City and Aston Villa to sign Wee Alex from Preston in 1929. The fee was a record £9,000, but it was money well spent as he inspired Arsenal to achieve their most successful spell in the history of the club.

Before he arrived The Gunners hadn't won a trophy, but in eight years he guided them to four League titles and three FA Cup Finals.

NERS

FRANK McLINTOCK
403 games 32 goals

INSPIRATIONAL captain whose greatest moments with Arsenal were courtesy of an inspirational move by Don Howe, then Arsenal's coach, who converted McLintock from a wing half into a centre-half following their disastrous League Cup Final defeat by Swindon in 1968.

Until then McLintock had been to Wembley four times and always finished on the losing side. He was known as soccer's biggest loser. But glory was around the corner when, in 1971, he skippered Arsenal to the League and Cup double.

McLintock, at 5ft 8ins, thought he was too small to operate as a centre-half, but his knowledge of the game and ability on the ball made him a formidable barrier at the heart of defence. Arsenal landed the European Fairs Cup (now the UEFA Cup) in 1970, their first trophy in 17 years, before lifting the double. Another personal triumph was to follow, when McLintock was awarded the MBE in 1972, and many Arsenal fans still believe he was sold too early when Bertie Mee transferred him to QPR in 1973.

DAVID O'LEARY

ONLY time will decide how many of George Graham's present side join the ranks of Highbury greats, but central defender David O'Leary has already reserved his place in the club's history.

Ireland's gentle giant has played in more first team games for the club than anyone, beating George Armstrong's record of 621 matches in 1989.

O'Leary was a member of the terrific trio along with Liam Brady and Frank Stapleton who went to the club from Dublin shortly after the double triumph of 1971. But unlike his pals, who later left the club, David was happy to continue his career with the club he loved despite several lucrative offers.

His loyalty was rewarded firstly in 1986 with a testimonial match against Celtic and then, three years later, with a Championship medal O'Leary feared would always elude him. And for many Highbury fans the most vivid memory of that dramatic night at Anfield, when Michael Thomas' last minute goal clinched the title, will always be the tears of joy that trickled down O'Leary's face.

CHARLIE GEORGE
179 games 49 goals

FEW players in Arsenal's glorious history had such a rapport with the North Bank, and not only because he spent his schooldays as a fan on the Highbury terraces. Charlie thrilled the fans with his natural ability.

Showmanship was also a big factor in Charlie's game, and that was never better illustrated than in the 1971 FA Cup Final when, after hitting a fantastic 20 yarder goal against Liverpool, he laid on the Wembley turf with his arms aloft to commemorate the moment. It is perhaps the most vivid memory of Arsenal's double that season.

Charlie was only 20 when he became a national celebrity that day, but his head-strong personality led to frequent arguments with manager Bertie Mee and, in 1976, he was sold to Derby County.

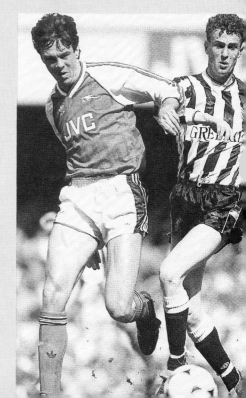

DEAR OLD PALS

BEST buddies Bryan Gunn (above) and Robert Fleck (above, right) couldn't believe it when they were re-united at Norwich.

The pair were friends, as well as rivals, when they were North of the border with Aberdeen and Rangers respectively.

They became colleagues at Carrow Road in December, 1987, when Fleck quit Ibrox in a £580,000 deal, while Gunn moved from Pittodrie for £100,000 the previous year.

Their friendship blossomed after they first lined up against each other at reserve level. "I remember scoring a penalty past the big man," grins goal ace Fleck.

"Robert likes to bring that up every now and again," laughs Gunn. "But I shut him up by reminding him about the result – 5-1 to The Dons!"

Fleck, who starred for Scotland in the 1990 World Cup is still counting the cost of staying with Gunn when he first arrived in East Anglia.

"Robert lodged with me for about five months and spent a small fortune. Neither of us could cook so we used to eat out," recalls Gunn.

"We used to toss a coin to decide who would pay and I must have come out on top about 90 per cent of the time!"

Now the pair are neighbours in a quiet estate just outside Norwich. Fleck lives with girlfriend Jane and one-year-old Olivia, while Gunn and wife Susan also have a daughter, Francesca.

NORWICH CITY

GORDON CONFESSES

IT'S confession time for Norwich star Dale Gordon, a boyhood fan of East Anglia rivals Ipswich.

"When Ipswich won the FA Cup in 1978 I cried for joy," admits the flying winger who was just 11 years old at the time. Now, at 24, he is The Canaries' longest-serving player, already a veteran of more than 250 senior games.

MIDFIELD man Tim Sherwood is hoping to attract the attention of England manager Graham Taylor all over again.

Taylor was in charge at Watford when Sherwood launched his career in the game and now he'd like a reunion with his former boss – at international level.

The 22-year-old has been a revelation since joining Norwich in the 1989 close season, proving a real snip at £170,000.

Sherwood's goalscoring record has been particularly impressive since joining The Canaries and he has regularly demonstrated his versatility by standing in as a central defender.

He has already earned recognition with the England Under-21 side and says: "It would be a big leap to the B or senior international tams, but you never know what might be around the corner."

TIM'S ENGLAND TARGET

VENNERS FURY

JOHN Polston's move to Norwich in the 1990 close season left Tottenham boss Terry Venables fuming.

The reason for Tel's anger was that a transfer tribunal pegged the young defender's fee at £300,000 – less than half what the Spurs boss was asking.

Venables' valuation was £750,000 and he argued: "When was the last time a young centre-half moved from one First Division club to another for less than £450,000?"

The young Londoner's rapid progress at Carrow Road merely reinforced Tel's view that Norwich had landed themselves a real bargain.

But there's nothing unusual about that. Ian Culverhouse, Mark Bowen and Ian Crook also quit White Hart Lane at knockdown prices to make a name for themselves with The Canaries.

Polston, 23, has no regrets. "It was a wrench to leave Spurs, but I knew I had to get away for the sake of my career. I wanted first team football and I've proved it was the best thing I could have done," he explains.

KENNY DALGLISH

It is supremely ironic that the footballer who is arguably the greatest ever Celtic player was, in fact, a Rangers fan in his youth. He even had to tear down posters of his Ibrox heroes when a Celtic scout went to the Dalglish home to persuade young Kenny to join the Parkhead club.

It was worth the effort. In 328 matches for Celtic, Dalglish bodyswerved his way round defenders to score 199 goals, helping the club win five League Championships, four Scottish Cups and one League Cup.

He is also the only man to win 100 caps for Scotland and, with Denis Law, shares the record for the number of goals scored for his country.

Dalglish's achievements at Parkhead are enough to overshadow 99 per cent of footballers, but it is a measure of his skill and dedication to the game that he won another bagful of honours when he left Parkhead for Liverpool in 1977.

JIMMY JOHNSTONE

Jimmy Johnstone was the Paul Daniels of football – a true magician who could send a whole crowd the wrong way with one of his amazing feints and dribbles.

Yet Johnstone, like George Best, was his own worst enemy because of a curious self-destruct button that tragically cut short his career in the game.

He still managed to win nine League Championship, a European Cup, four Scottish Cup, and five League Cup medals during his days at Parkhead.

Johnstone was fearless on the pitch, but used to shake like a leaf at the thought of flying in an aircraft. And it was his phobia of flying that provided the background to what was arguably his greatest performance for the club.

Celtic were playing Red Star Belgrade at home in the first leg of a European Cup tie in 1968, and manager Jock Stein promised Johnstone he wouldn't have to travel to the away leg if he could inspire the Celts to a comfortable lead at home.

Johnstone ripped through the Yugoslavs, scored twice and layed on three more goals in an incredible 7-2 victory. 'I don't need tae go, I don't need tae go,' exclaimed Jimmy as he danced off the pitch.

Neutrals who watch Celtic often ask why the players don't have numbers on the back of their shirts. Parkhead fans reply that everyone knows who the players in their famous green and white hoops are. Here we spotlight six Celtic greats who could have played with paper bags on their heads – and would still have been instantly recognisable.

BILLY McNEILL

Reserved a special place in Celtic's history when he became the first British player to hold aloft the European Cup as skipper in 1967.

Hailed as Caesar by his adoring Parkhead public, McNeill was a centre half who also holds the distinction of scoring in three Scottish Cup finals.

He played for a total of 17 seasons for Celtic, appearing in more than 80 games and winning 23 winners' medals – a total that is believed to be a world record.

No wonder he returned to the club at the end of his playing days to manage Celtic in 1978 until 1983, during which the club won three more League titles, and both the Scottish Cup and League Cup.

A spell in England followed in charge of Manchester City and Aston Villa, but McNeill returned to manage Celtic in time to lead them to a League and Cup double in 1988 – the club's Centenary.

PARKHEAD

PAUL McSTAY

His talent in midfield was such that McStay never played a reserve game for the club, but jumped from youth team to first- team to make his League debut against Aberdeen when he was 17.

Celtic beat off strong competition from Everton, Leeds and Tottenham for the footballer who has been called a Celtic supporter who also has a contract to play for the club.

That isn't meant as a slight against his ability, more an indication of his love affair with the club that also signed his brothers Willie and Raymond.

Paul's incredible skill was summed up by Billy McNeill, who said: "When Paul McStay plays, Celtic play."

DANNY McGRAIN

Seven of Danny's 20 seasons at Parkhead prompted many Scottish fans to argue he was the best right back in Europe.

And that is a remarkable feat when it is considered that his career was hampered by diabetes, a fractured skull and a broken leg.

Like Dalglish, McGrain preferred to watch Rangers as a schoolboy. But it is rumoured that Rangers passed up their chance to sign him because they thought, mistakenly, that he was a Catholic.

JOCK STEIN

The perfect example of how an ugly duckling can blossom into a swan … Jock was a strictly average footballer whose arrival at Parkhead was greeted by apathy among the fans.

He never won a Scotland cap, had no pace and only limited ability on the ball, but made up for that by his inspirational leadership both on and, most significantly, off the park.

Celtic were going through a barren spell when he arrived in 1951, and merely achieved sparodical success in the trophy stakes with him as their skipper.

But when he took over as manager in 1965 Stein came into his own, turning the club into Scotland's major force during 10 glorious years.

They won the title nine times on the trot, lifted the Scottish cup six times, the League Cup six times and, of course, the European Cup.

A crowd of 60,000 paid tribute to that achievement when they turned up for his testimonial match against Liverpool in 1978. Stein literally gave his life for football when, as manager of the Scotland side, he collapsed and died seconds after watching them qualify for the World Cup Finals in 1985.

SWEEPER

DID you know that many of today's top stars had very down-to-earth jobs before their careers hit the big-time?

SHOOT takes a look at the previous employment records of some of the game's leading players...

What do David Seaman, Stuart Pearce, Chris Waddle, Peter Beardsley and Ian Wright have in common — apart from the fact that they are all England internationals?

The answer is that they head a list of top British footballers who were nearly lost to the game altogether after they were forced to take up other employment.

Most of today's big-name stars kicked off their careers straight from school, picked out by talent-spotters and groomed for stardom from an early age.

But a large number had to wait a lot longer for their big chance. Waddle, for example, was working in a sausage skin factory when Newcastle United snapped him up.

He later moved to Tottenham and in 1989 he joined France outfit Marseilles for a massive £4.5 million — a British record deal.

Waddle's former Newcastle colleague, Peter Beardsley, was actually on the dole when he left school in the North East and it was several weeks later that he landed a job as a factory labourer.

Brighton's Robert Codner was an insurance agent.

BEARDSLEY

David Seaman – ex-baker's boy now in the dough with Arsenal

Former sausage maker Chris Waddle

Michael Cheetham soldiers on for Cambridge

He remembers: "I worked for a company who made valves for ships. My responsibilities included sweeping the floors, cleaning the machines and running errands such as fetching lunches from the chip shop."

Peter eventually quit the job to launch his career with Carlisle, then moved to Canadian club Vancouver Whitecaps and back to Newcastle before Liverpool snapped him up for £1.9 million in 1987.

Crystal Palace striker Ian Wright also spent time on the dole, in between spells as a labourer and plasterer, and played his football for non-league Greenwich Borough.

His life changed in 1985 when Palace took him on, and after helping them to promotion to the First Division he was rewarded with his international chance by England manager Graham Taylor.

Ian's Selhurst Park colleague, skipper Geoff Thomas, used to work as an electrician and played his football in the lower divisions with Rochdale and Crewe.

continued overleaf

He joined Palace in 1987 and within four years powered his way into England's senior squad alongside another former 'sparkie' in Nottingham Forest skipper Stuart Pearce.

David Seaman became the world's most expensive goalkeeper when he moved across London from Queen's Park Rangers to Arsenal in 1990 at a cost of £1.3 million.

That's a lot of dough for the former baker's boy who was shown the door by Leeds and had to rebuild his career at a lower level with Peterborough and Birmingham City.

The Linighan brothers, Andy and David, both finished apprenticeships before turning to football as a full-time career. Andy, who cost Arsenal £1.2 million from Norwich in 1990, is a qualified joiner, while Ipswich skipper David served his time as a plumber.

David's predecessor as Ipswich captain, Dutch international Romeo Zondervan, worked as a motor mechanic in Holland, while their Portman Road colleagues, Neil Thompson and Simon Milton, gave up their jobs as nappy salesman and paint sprayer to switch to football on a full-time basis.

Portsmouth paid the princely sum of £450 to buy ace marksman Guy Whittingham out of the Army, while midfield man Michael Cheetham cost Ipswich only £400 before they sold him to FA Cup giantkillers Cambridge United for £50,000.

England 'B' striker Paul Williams was an accounts clerk before Charlton Athletic lured him from Woodford Town in 1986. Four years later he was on his way to Sheffield Wednesday in a £600,000 deal.

Scotland's most capped goalkeeper, Jim Leighton, used to hand over unemployment benefit when he worked as a civil servant before joining Aberdeen and then later moving South to Manchester United.

Anglo Scots trio Ian Bryson, Bernie Slaven and Duncan Shearer all enjoyed the outdoor life North of the border. Ian was a farm worker before moving from Kilmarnock to Sheffield United, Bernie gave up his job as a gardener when Middlesbrough bought him from Albion Rovers, and Duncan quit an Inverness sawmill to try his luck with Chelsea, later moving to Huddersfield and then Swindon.

Celtic sharpshooter Tommy Coyne, who cost £500,000 from Dundee in 1989, started his working life as a joiner, while Old Firm rival Ian

Ferguson was a hospital porter and also had a stint delivering soft drinks.

John Colquhoun was a painter and decorator before joining Celtic and then moving to Hearts, while his Tynecastle colleague, goalkeeper Henry Smith, is an ex-miner.

Up at Aberdeen, defender Brian Grant is a former bank clerk, midfield man Craig Robertson was a production controller at a factory where they turned out satellite dishes, and striker Willem van der Ark was an insurance agent as was Brighton's midfielder Robert Codner.

Dundee striker Keith Wright was a cashier for a firm of estate agents, while his Tayside rival, Darren Jackson of Dundee United, worked as a printer.

And much-travelled former Scotland striker Steve Archibald, whose career has taken him to Clyde, Aberdeen, Tottenham, Barcelona, Hibs, Espanol and St. Mirren, actually picked up his first wage packet as a motor mechanic.

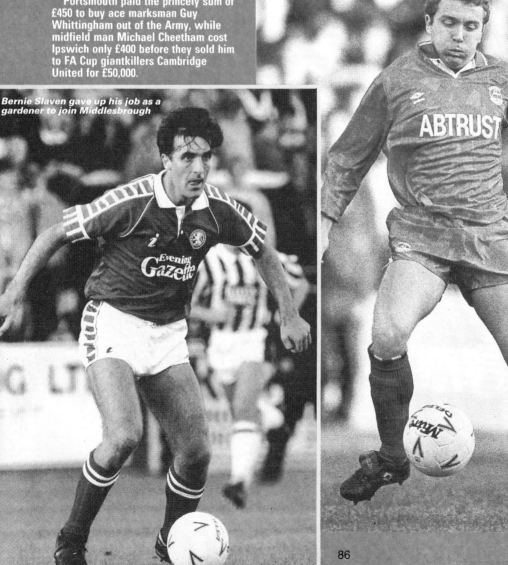

Craig Robertson turned
satellite dishes

Bernie Slaven gave up his job as a gardener to join Middlesbrough

GARY McALLISTER
Leeds Utd

GRANNY SMITH'S TIPS FOR THE TOP

Hi, Granny Smith here. Now British clubs are back in Europe I'm here to pass on some tips for all fans following their teams abroad.

EUROPEAN TRAVELS

1 You'll need a passport

2 For some reason English money can't be used in the rest of Europe. So take some foreign lolly like Franks, Potatoes and Dutch Builders.

3 Don't eat abroad.

4 Take a translation book as a number of Europeans can't understand English, especially Geordie accents. Mind you most Britons can't understand the Geordies.

5 Only sleep in a bed

6 Don't mention the war.

7 Call all Germans Hans.

8 Call all Frenchmen Pierre.

9 Make sure you either fly or go by boat as there is some water to cross.

10 Don't come back.

Hope you have a good journey.

Gran

A Coal Porter Classic
The Referee

See me
Hear me
Don't touch me
I am the referee

I watch you
Kick the opposition
I watch you
Treat me with derision

I get my card
Out of my shirt
And watch you walk
As you lose your smirk

I see you dive
Here and there
I think you're cheating
And that's not fair

I blow my whistle
And stop the game
But the crowd and TV
Give me the blame

I try my best
To be a good referee
So don't be too hard
On little old me

JOKE SPOT

QUESTION:
What's the connection between pop star Michael Jackson and Scottish goalkeepers?

ANSWER:
They both wear gloves for no apparent reason.

FASHION FRO

The loose hanging with mini skirt

Fed up with the boring kits footballers wear today? We are so we contacted top Italian designer Pietro Gucci and asked him to design the kits of tomorrow.

The off-the-shoulder with frills look

The stylish page boy surfer

THE THINGS THEY SAY

I can't watch Wimbledon, Sheffield Wednesday or Watford. Football wasn't meant to be run by two linesmen and air traffic control. **Tommy Docherty, 1988**

John Ebbrell's shin pad is going in to hospital tonight. We'll ask for a new one for the replay. **Howard Kendall talking about Steve McMahon's controversial tackle on the Everton defender in last season's FA Cup Fifth Round meeting.**

I think Iraq are finding it a problem at the moment, too. **Norwich boss Dave Stringer after it was suggested his side was suspect in the air last season.**

I'm disappointed not to have played but I'm a superstar and deserve to be paid. **Roger Milla after refusing to play for Cameroon in their 2-0 defeat by England at Wembley last season because the FA wouldn't pay his £50,000 appearance fee.**

While I was in Rio a photographer asked me to juggle a ball on the Copacabana beach. I felt so embarrassed – we were surrounded by kids who could juggle the ball so much better than me. **John Barnes**

I was in this disco when this short fat guy came up and hugged me. It was only when I noticed his bodyguard that I realised it was Diego Maradona. **Ruud Gullit**

It's easy enough to get to Ireland. Just a short walk across the Irish Sea as far as I'm concerned. **Brian Clough**

I don't know what this nice guy tag means. Do you have to be nasty to be a manager? **Trevor Francis when boss at QPR.**

He was taking pictures of my bad side. **Joe Royle after soaking a photographer with a bucket of water at Oldham's 1-1 draw at Charlton last season.**

CKS

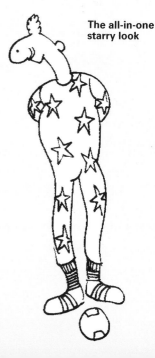

The all-in-one starry look

The baggy shorts with matching hat and braces

The Pom Pom with frilly shorts

It seems that every soccer star fancies himself as the next George Michael. First there was the 1970 England World Cup squad with their touching rendition of 'Back Home', then Kevin Keegan hit the charts with 'Head Over Heels In Love', Chris Waddle and Glenn Hoddle followed up with the instantly forgettable 'Diamond Lights' and even Gazza got in the act with his 'foot-tappy' Top Ten hit 'Fog On The Tyne'.

So we asked SHOOT readers to come up with ten records that could be hits for the soccer players of today. Here is a selection of the best and there's T-shirts on the way to our Top Ten:

A brother and sister double act in the form of Nicole and Russell Palmer are right on key with this collection of hits:

Gonna Make You Sweat – FIFA on their bid to get referees fitter
Missing You – Spurs to Chris Waddle
Falling – Aston Villa
Wicked Game – Punch-up kings Arsenal and Manchester United
Fantasy – Woking
Crazy – Vinny Jones
It Takes Two – Ian Wright and Mark Bright
Coming Out Of The Dark – Ian and Alan Knight (get it!)
Being Boring – George Graham
Ghost Town – Wimbledon

David Jones of Harold Hill in Essex is playing the right melody with:

In The Family – Clive, Paul, Bradley and Martin Allen
Substitute – Andy Linighan
I Won't Bleed For You – Lee Chapman
Innocent – Jimmy Case to George Courtney after his sending-off last season.
Father And Son – The Cloughs
Money For Nothing – Tony Cascarino
In The Air Tonight – Wimbledon
Oldest Swinger In Town – Peter Shilton
Shaddup Your Face – Referees to Gazza
Can't Stand Losing You – Tottenham to Gazza

Tony Fearon of Co.Armagh, Northern Ireland has hit the right note with these little numbers:

Don't Stand So Close To Me – Gazza to Vinny
Boogie Nights – Mo Johnston
Born In The USA – John Harkes
Money For Nothing – Roger Milla
Son Of My Father – Nigel Clough
My Way – Jack Charlton
I Don't Like Mondays – Halifax managers
We Are Family – The Allens
I Can't Stand Losing You – Liverpool on the League Championship
Walking Tall – Niall Quinn

Robert and David Spowart aren't Brothers Beyond coming up with Soccer Singalongs. Just look at these dodgy discs:

Bring Your Daughter To The Slaughter – Vinny Jones
Head Over Heels – Hugo Sanchez
Won't Talk About It – Kenny Dalglish

SOCCER Singa

Andy Mynott, an Arsenal fan from Saffron Walden in Essex, hit the Top Ten with this chart buster:

Every Loser Wins – Sheffield United
Land of Confusion – Liverpool era – between Dalglish and Souness
Papa Don't Preach – Nigel Clough
U Can't Touch This – Brian Clough to Juventus re Des Walker
King Of Emotion – Gazza
Speed Demon – Lee Sharpe
You Keep Me Hanging On – Neville Southall to Everton
Faith – Halifax Supporters Club
Get Up! – Anders Limpar
Goldfinger – Ron Atkinson

Three Warwickshire girls, Claire Smith, Caroline Lambert and Katie Lyne, have formed a trio to bring you this hit parade.

Dirty Cash – Swindon
Don't Worry Be Happy – Kenny Dalglish
Wild Thing – Vinny Jones
Leader Of The Pack – Bryan Robson
Better The Devil You Know – Manchester United
What's The Colour of Money? – Roger Milla
Straight Up – Sheffield Wednesday
The Only Way Is Up – Aldershot
Living On A Prayer – Tottenham's accountant
The Wanderer – John (11 club) Burridge

John Burridge – The Wanderer.

Crazy Thing – Keith Hackett after sending-off West Ham's Tony Gale in last season's FA Cup Semi-Final
Almost Felt Like Crying – Tony Gale after the above incident
International Bright Young Thing – England's Ian Wright
I'm Your Number One – Chris Woods to Graham Taylor
I Am The One And Only – Brian Clough
Ain't No Stopping Us Now – Arsenal
Straight Up – Niall Quinn

Jack Blanchard of Anglesey in Wales has 'em singing in the valleys with:

I Only Want To Be With You – Steve Bull to Wolves
Getting Better All The Time – Sheffield United
Hangin' Tough – Wimbledon
Shot Down In A Blaze Of Glory – Woking
Four Letter Word – Gazza
Ordinary Angel – Gary Lineker
I've Missed Again – Charlton striker Carl Leaburn (4 goals in over 70 League games)

Don't Stand So Close To Me – Vinny!

Reet Petite – Dennis Wise
The Great Pretender – Jurgen Klinsmann
Dreamin' – Andy Dibble when he let in Gary Crosby for that goal a couple of seasons ago
Calling All The Heroes – Manchester United
Land Of Confusion – AC Milan and Marseille after the lights went out in their European Cup match last season
Get Here – Lazio to Gazza
Back Where We Belong – Arsenal

Marguerite Doran of Bagenalstown, Co. Carlow in Ireland is on song with this selection:

Tears of a Clown – Paul Gascoigne
Freedom – Tony Adams
Disappear – Wimbledon fans
Money Talks – Tottenham
Cry For Help – Derby
Can I Kick It? – Terry Hurlock
Summer's Magic – Jack Charlton and the Republic of Ireland
Couldn't Say Goodbye – Mo Johnston to Scotland
Wiggle It – Cameroon World Cup star Roger Milla (above)
Someday – Manchester United on their Championship hopes

One More Chance – Scotland to Mo Johnston
Sometimes – John Barnes
Never Going To Give You Up – Arsenal to David O'Leary

The Welsh are said to have an ear for good music and Nathan Edwards of Glamorgan is obviously no exception.

Speed Demon – Tony Daley
Pass The Dutchie On the Left Hand Side – Ruud Gullit
Don't Cry For Me Argentina – Diego Maradona
It's A Shame – Swindon
Enjoy The Silence – Wimbledon fans
Back Where We Belong – Liverpool on Europe
Get Up – Jurgen Klinsmann
Rescue Me – Andy Linighan on his Arsenal troubles
When The Going Gets Tough – Steve McMahon
What Do I Have To Do? – Chris Waddle to Graham Taylor

Keith Hodge of Paignton in Devon brings music to our ears with this hit parade:

Should I Stay Or Should I Go – Gazza
Downtown – Halifax Town
Don't Give Up – Rangers to the rest of Scottish football

Don't Cry For Me Diego.

***T**HE ultimate Christmas present for any Celtic and Rangers fan would be the sort of job filled by Jim Steel and George Soutar.*

Both are in their seventies, and support Celtic and Rangers respectively. But they are the envy of the thousands of other Old Firm fans. Instead of watching every match from the terraces or the stands, Steel and Soutar can be found with the players in the dressing-room, or in the touchline dug-out.

Every club has a figure such as Steel or Soutar on its backroom staff. The basic jobs of these men is to cater for the players' needs; to ensure the players have the kit they want, for example, and make the tea. Their role can also be described as a cross between that of a court jester and agony aunt. This is particularly true in the cases of Steel and Soutar ....

OLD FIRM RIV

GEORGE SOUTAR, the Rangers' kit man, is treated like a favourite uncle by the young Ibrox stars.

Ally McCoist goes out with him socially, the pair have even been known to go to discos together, and when Derek Ferguson was at the club, he and Ian Durrant went on holiday with him.

Soutar, a widower who has seven grandchildren, insists that he has achieved the ultimate in job satisfaction.

He was born and raised in the street alongside Ibrox and has supported the club since he was a small boy. "I never felt the need to ask for autographs, because I saw the players every day," he recalls. But it is only in recent years that he has got close to their stars again.

A bricklayer by trade, the tiny Soutar, nicked 'Doddy', spent four largely tedious, unfulfilled years in retirement before he got the chance to join the backroom staff at Rangers.

He was brought there by David Holmes, the chief executive of the John Lawrence building group which then owned the club and which had employed Soutar for more than 30 years. "It saved my life," George recalls. "It gave me a reason for getting up in the morning."

His role, as the Rangers players' general factotum, is not without its problems.

The players take delight in increasing his work load to the extent of causing him to mutter darkly under his breath. "Do you think I am here to run around after you lot?" he'll ask. "Yes," they retort.

Graham Roberts, one of Soutar's favourites when he was at Ibrox, once playfully kicked the ball at him in the dressing-room. It shattered his glasses and cut his nose.

There was also the occasion when Soutar, having volunteered to go in goal to make up the numbers of a Rangers practice match, came out of a challenge with Roberts with a damaged hand.

He had to go to hospital and, even worse, explain how the injury had occurred.

"You should have seen the expression on the nurse's face when I told her I had been playing football with the Rangers players.

"I was there for about an half and a half, and people kept poking their heads around the door to look at me. I think they were considering whether I should be taken to the local asylum."

George Soutar.

Jim Steel.

"They like to confide in me, tell me about all their little worries," says Steel, a bachelor who has been with the club for more than 35 years.

They also play all manner of practical jokes on him. Hence the fact that, when he is with the Celtic or Scotland team in foreign parts, he hides his false teeth. He has been thrown in to swimming pools more times than he can remember.

Not surprisingly, Steel, who does not smoke or drink and is a great believer in taking vitamin tables, remains as lively in body and mind as someone a quarter of his age.

He learned his massage skills as a PTI in the RAF in the 1930's. He was stationed in Wiltshire and when Freddie Mills, the boxer, was moved there, he became Mills' trainer.

Steel was then approached by the then Celtic manager, Jimmy McStay. "Originally, I just went to help out at Parkhead when I was on leave," he recalls. "but the involvement just grew and grew."

Steel, reasonably well off financially through his involvement in a family drapery business, has become one of the most popular characters in the game. Being with him in the dressing-room before a match is one of the highlights of the week for Celtic's players.

In addition to giving each man a rub-down with warm olive oil, he is also noted for a little cabaret act comprising a take-off of a flamboyant horse racing tipster who once held court in a Glasgow square each Sunday morning.

One of the most celebrated stories told about Steel concerns a match against Liverpool at Anfield, when Reds boss Bill Shankly walked in to the Celtic dressing-room to deliver his customary opposition wind-up.

"Shut the door, Mr Shankly," Steel shouted, having just finished his last massage. "The bees (players) are buzzing in here. They are so red hot, you'll need to call the fire brigade."

Even Shankly was stuck for a reply. "Oh, welcome, lads," he muttered, and walked out.

ALS

JIM STEEL, Celtic and Scotland's team masseur, has had offers to join forces with many of the top managers in Scotland. Graeme Souness even tried to lure him to Rangers before he left Ibrox for Liverpool.

There are not many men in professional football with his massage skills. There are certainly not many with his sense of humour and ability to ease dressing-room tension before big games.

As the former Celtic captain, Danny McGrain, says: "Players have always flocked to his treatment bench like moths attracted to a flame."

The ultimate for Jim and George ... watching a no-holes barred, typical full-blooded Celtic v Rangers clash.

WORLD

Tackle these questions on the stars of world football.

ANSWERS ON PAGE 121

1 In which position does Lothar Matthaus (above) play?

2 Against which country did Italy's Roberto Baggio score the Goal of the 1990 World Cup finals?

3 Enzo Scifo is the midfield playmaker for which European country?

4 For which French club does Jean-Pierre Papin play?

5 Colourful Colombian Carlos Valderrama was in action for which club against Manchester United in last season's European Cup-Winners' Cup?

6 Romanian star Gheorghe Hagi (below, right) plays for Inter Milan, Real Madrid or Marseille?

7 AC Milan turned in one of the best club displays in world football in their 4-0 win over Steaua Bucharest in the 1989 European Cup Final. Which two Dutch players scored twice?

8 How many League seasons did Ian Rush (right) spend in Italy with Juventus?

9 Which record breaking Danish international managed Brondby in their UEFA Cup quest last season?

10 What is the nickname of Italian striker Salvatore Schillaci?

11 Which record did Italy's Walter Zenga (below) beat during the 1990 World Cup?

12 Who were the opposition when Careca scored his first goal for Brazil in the 1990 World Cup finals?

13 For which West German club has Mark Hughes played League football?

14 Tomas Brolin is an international for Denmark, Finland, Norway or Sweden?

15 For which Spanish club does Bernd Schuster play?

SOCCER

QUIZ

16 Was Paul Gascoigne with Newcastle or Tottenham when he made his senior England debut?

17 He plays in midfield for Red Star Belgrade and is one of the most talented youngsters in international football. Who is he?

18 Can you name the Argentine 'keeper who became a hero in the summer of 1990?

19 Aston Villa's Paul McGrath was voted Man of the Match in which FA Cup Final?

20 Why did Marseille's £5 million signing Dragan Stojkovic endure a miserable time last season?

21 Paul McStay (above, right) made his debut for Scotland against Uruguay in 1980, 1984 or 1986?

22 There are three West Germans at Inter Milan. Matthaus and Jurgen Klinsmann are two. Who is the other?

23 In which spectacular way has Hugo Sanchez scored a number of goals?

24 For which country does goalkeeper Taffarel (right) play?

25 How many goals did Claudio Caniggia (below) score for Argentina in the 1990 World Cup finals?

MORE FOOTBALL
FUNNIES

"The new bloke, a bit of an exhibitionist – isn't he?"

"Come on – own up – who put the superglue on the ball?"

"He's busy at the moment – exercising his finger for this afternoon's match –"

"You were supposed to have played your last match last Saturday –"

"It was a real laugh – you walked into the goal post and broke your nose – stepped back on the ball and broke your ankle – fell off the stretcher and broke your arm – have a grape –"

"Before you allow that penalty, ref – my boss wants you on the phone –"

EARL

BARRETT

OLDHAM

STEEL CITY

Blades back

Sheffield can now boast two top flight clubs for the first time in 23 years – and two of the most charismatic managers.

The last time United met Wednesday in a First Division fixture was back in 1968, and much of the credit for the resurgence of soccer in the steel city must go to Dave Bassett and Ron Atkinson.

Bassett has worked wonders at Bramall Lane over the past few years, particularly last season when he hauled them back from the brink of relegation … and humiliation.

After 16 First Division games, the Blades had amassed just four League points and looked certs for the drop.

But, from their last 22 games they added another 42 points to avoid relegation by a comfortable margin to finish in a creditable 13th place.

Meanwhile, across the city, Ron Atkinson was skilfully guiding Wednesday back to Division One – collecting the Rumbelows Cup in the process.

Now the two larger than life figures are locked in a head-to-head battle for supremacy in the soccer mad city. Yet, for so long, it had looked odds on that by the end of the

UNITED FAX

Ground: Bramall Lane, Sheffield S2 4SU
Capacity: 35,618
Record attendance: 68,287 v Leeds, 1936
Nickname: The Blades
Manager: Dave Bassett
Year formed: 1889
Record League victory: 10-0 v Burslem Port Vale, 1892
Record Cup victory: 5-0 v Newcastle, 1914; 5-0 v Corinthians, 1925; 5-0 v Barrow, 1956
Record defeat: 0-13 v Bolton, 1890
Most League goals in a season: 102 – Division One, 1925-26
Highest League scorer in a season: Jimmy Dunne – 41, 1930-31
Most League goals (aggregate): Harry Johnson – 205, 1919-30
Most capped player: Billy Gillespie – 25, Northern Ireland
Most League appearances: Joe Shaw – 629, 1948-66
Record transfer fee paid: £700,000 to Leeds for Vinnie Jones, 1990
Football League record: 1892 elected to Division Two; 1893-1934 Division One; 1934-39 Division Two; 1946-49 Division One; 1949-53 Division Two; 1953-56 Division One; 1956-61 Division Two; 1961-68 Division One; 1968-71 Division Two; 1971-76 Division One; 1976-79 Division Two; 1979-81 Division Three; 1981-82 Division Four; 1982-84 Division Three; 1984-88 Division Two; 1988-89 Division Three; 1989-90 Division Two; 1990-Division One.
Honours: Division One Champions 1897-98; runners-up 1896-97, 1899-1900; Division Two Champions – 1952-53; runners-up 1892-93, 1938-39, 1960-61, 1970-71, 1989-90; Division Four Champions 1981-82; FA Cup winners 1899, 1902, 1915, 1925; runners-up 1901, 1936.

SHOWDOWN

nd Owls are n business

Wednesday boss Ron Atkinson. Below: Paul Williams (No.10) celebrates his late winner against Bristol City.

season they would again pass each other on the road in and out of the First Division.

Bassett however, despite his club's apalling start to last season, was never in doubt that United would maintain their First Division status.

"Even when the rest of the League was writing us off, I knew we could avoid the drop," he insists. "I have been in relegation battles with Wimbledon and Watford and I can smell relegation. But there wasn't even a sniff at Bramall Lane.

"It took the players some time to come to terms with the First Division. Most of them had never played there before. But we're better for the experience and hopefully days of survival are behind us."

Bassett's opposite number over at Hillsborough, Ron Atkinson, has nothing but praise and admiration for the United chief and says: "He's done a wonderful job and you have to take your hat off to him."

Wednesday fans too are are more than happy to doff their flat caps to the Hillsborough boss who led the club back to the top flight after just one season away.

A Wembley victory over his old club Manchester United in the Rumbelows Cup was the icing on the cake for Big Ron, who now has his sights set on even greater things.

"I would love nothing more than to bring European football back to Hillsborough," he proclaims. "Playing the likes of Barcelona or Juventus may be some way off, but what's wrong with thinking big?"

WEDNESDAY FAX

Ground: Hillsborough, Sheffield S6 1SW
Capacity: 38,780
Record attendance: 72,841 v Man.City, 1934
Nickname: The Owls
Manager: Ron Atkinson
Year formed: 1867 (fifth oldest League club)
Record League victory: 9-1 v Birmingham, 1930
Record Cup victory: 12-0 v Halliwell, 1891
Record defeat: 0-10 v Aston Villa, 1912
Most League goals: 106 – Division Two, 1958-59
Highest League scorer in a season: Derek Dooley – 46, 1951-52
Most League goals (aggregate): Andy Wilson – 199, 1900-20
Most capped player: Ron Springett – 33, England
Most League appearances: Andy Wilson – 502, 1900-20
Record transfer fee paid: £750,000 to West Brom for Carlton Palmer, 1989
Football League record: 1892 elected to Division One; 1899-1900 Division Two; 1900-22 Division One; 1920-26 Division Two; 1926-37 Division One; 1937-50 Division Two; 1950-51 Division One; 1951-52 Division Two; 1952-55 Division One; 1955-56 Division Two; 1956-58 Division One; 1958-59 Division Two; 1959-70 Division One; 1970-75 Division Two; 1975-80 Divison Three; 1980-84 Division Two; 1984-90 Divison One; 1990-91 Division Two; 1991 – Division One.
Honours: Division One Champions 1902-03, 1903-04, 1928-29, 1929-30; runners-up 1960-61; Division Two Champions 1899-1900, 1925-26, 1951-52, 1955-56, 1958-59; runners-up 1949-50, 1983-84. FA Cup winners 1896, 1907, 1935; runners-up 1890, 1966.

G*O*A*L!

Ronnie Whelan dives to head home Liverpool's matchwinner at Wimbledon.

Nottingham Forest skipper Stuart Pearce crashes this free-kick past the Manchester United wall to score at Old Trafford.

Trevor Morley (on ground, right) scores for West Ham in a 3-1 victory over Millwall at Upton Park.

Nigel Pearson scores spectacularly for Sheffield Wednesday against Ipswich.

Paul Mason (on ground) scores a great goal for Aberdeen in a 3-2 win over Dunfermline at Pittodrie. Andy Rhodes is the out of luck 'keeper.

G*O*A*L!

SAVES  of the

Sunderland 'keeper Tony Norman stops Arsenal's David Rocastle from scoring at Highbury.

Celtic's Pat Bonner handles this Rangers attack in last season's Skol Cup Final.

Gary Lineker finds Arsenal's David Seaman a formidable barrier at White Hart Lane.

SEASON

St Johnstone's Lindsay Hamilton saves on the line from Motherwell striker Iain Ferguson.

Erik Thorstvedt makes a crucial save for Spurs against Arsenal in the FA Cup Semi-Final at Wembley.

Even Peter Shilton's safe hands couldn't prevent Derby County from relegation last season.

CZECH MATE!

The popular John Burridge was released by Newcastle.

NEWCASTLE UNITED 'keeper Pavel Srnicek is not one to go along with the view that there's no sentiment in soccer.

The 24-year-old Pavel, a one-time Czech soldier, said a personal sorry to 39-year-old John Burridge, the veteran goalkeeper who was given a free transfer by Newcastle United manager Ossie Ardiles at the end of last season and replaced by Srnicek.

"I owe Budgie a lot," says Srnicek. "We spent a lot of time together in training and he helped me tremendously when I first arrived at the club last January.

"Although I felt sorry for John when he told me he was leaving the club, I realised the chance was there for me to establish myself. It's all part of the game, and my job, to try to make sure I'm successful with United.

"First I had to prove myself to Jim Smith, who showed faith in me when he brought me here, and now I've to do it for Ossie Ardiles."

Adjusted

Srnicek was bought for £350,000 from Banik Ostrava, and quickly adjusted to life in the North East. But he realises how important the immediate future is to his career.

He says: "I'm ambitious for success, and if I do well with Newcastle it would help me in my ambition to make a bid for a place in Czechoslovakia's 1994 World Cup squad."

Srnicek hopes his progress since he arrived at St. James has been duly noted abroad. "There's a lot of interest in English football in my country."

JOHN DREYER
LUTON

Give that man a hand! Portsmouth goalkeeper Andy Gosney obviously has a lot of faith in his defence. Ah well, everyone knows 'keepers are crazy.

Bored with ripping defences to shreds with his feet, Gary Lineker has come up with an alternative.

SNAF

The youngsters at Dundee United have got all the good jobs – now they've got to model for Maurice Malpas. Tell him to turn the camera round the right way, lads.

There you are, what did I say .... now Bruce Grobbelaar has gone over the top – he's adopted the Gazza tongue look.

BELHAVEN

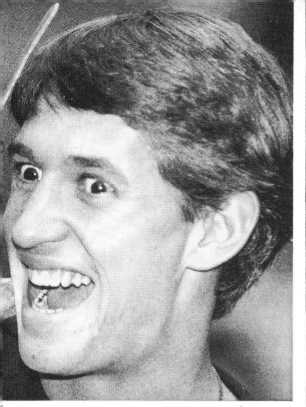

SHOTS

Hah, now let's see Ray Houghton and his Liverpool mates score with these.

Someone tell Paul Parker he is meant to put his shorts on before the game.

THE new Women's National Premier League which kicks off this season brings together eight top sides including the 1991 Mycil Women's F.A. Cup Finalists, Doncaster Belles, and Millwall Lionesses.

The League will help England's manager and ex-Sutton United boss, Barrie Williams, pick his best squad for England's fifth UEFA encounter and to become a force to be reckoned with in the world.

This new League venture is a far cry from those days back in the 1880's when women only participated in football to raise money for charity. Although by 1917 factory sides in Lancashire were playing to raise funds specifically for War charities.

Some time later, one of these 'factory' sides Preston Ladies, nicknamed "Dick Keer's" after the big engineering works there, represented England and became World Champions for many years. They eventually disbanded in 1965.

When England's men won the World Cup in 1966 it had an unexpected knock on effect – more girls and women took up the game and a series of Leagues were formed.

It soon became apparent competitive women's football needed to be organised. So in November 1969 the Women's Football Association was formed with 44 affiliated clubs.

The W.F.A. is now in its 21st year, and can boast a membership of 8,000 registered players, 342 clubs and 19 Leagues.

The standard of women's football is now progressing in skills at both domestic and international level and is producing the likes of the Doncaster Belles, who won last season's League Championship for the 13th year.

This national Premier League can improve the standard further.

National Premier League will help our girls become a world force...

WOND
WOM

Milestones

1917 – Fund-raising games played in aid of War charities.

1943 – Matches organised to help War effort.

1965 – "Dick Kerr's" Preston Ladies disband. During its 800 game history the club had represented England and for many years had been undisputed World Champions.

1967 – Women more interested in organised football after England's success in the World Cup led to more women joining clubs.

1969 – Women's Football Association formed with 44 clubs.

1970 – Following W.F.A. representation to the F.A., 1921 rule banning women from playing organised football is rescinded. Women's teams are allowed to play on F.A. pitches.

1971 – FIFA and UEFA recognise the women's game and encourage members to implement measures for its proper control. Southampton win the first ever Women's F.A. Cup Final beating Stewarton & Thistle 4-1.

1972 – W.F.A. form an England international side. In their first ever match they defeat Scotland 3-2.

1980 – The W.F.A. and the F.A. form a Joint Consultative Committee to develop the game. Official W.F.A. headquarters is established in London.

1982 – The Women's European Championships are inaugurated.

1984 – England reach the final of the

FINAL FACTS

★ Photos show action from the 1991 Mycil Women's Cup Final played at Tranmere.

★ Millwall Lionesses defeated odds-on favourite Doncaster Belles 1-0.

★ Match winner was Yvonne Baldeo who scored in the 65th minute.

★ Attendance was 4,010.

European Championships losing 4-3 on penalties to Sweden. The W.F.A. affiliated to the F.A.

1985 – England win a mini-World Cup 'Mundialito' tournament by defeating the host nation, Italy 3-2 in the Final.

1987 – England reach the Semi-Finals of the European Championships, but lose again to Sweden after extra-time.

1988 – For the second time, England win the 'Mundialito' tournament.

1989 – 2.5 million watch the Women's F.A. Cup highlights on Channel Four TV which was staged at Man. United's Old Trafford ground with Liverpool's Leasowe Pacific running out as 3-2 victors over Friends of Fulham. The first full women's match (England 0-2 Sweden) staged at Wembley Stadium as a curtain raiser to the men's Rous Cup match with highlights shown on BBC Sportsnight.

Michelle Cockburn becomes first woman to hold a full F.A. coaching badge and is appointed as Development officer for the North West.

The W.F.A. membership grows to include 21 Leagues plus nine regional Leagues, over 250 clubs and 8,000 registered players.

Linda Whitehead, Secretary of the W.F.A., is awarded by *The Sunday Times* "Sports Administrator of the Year".

1990 – William Hill bookmakers announce first ever odds on the 1989/90 W.F.A. Cup competition.

Channel Four TV shows four hours of U.E.F.A. and W.F.A. Cup football.

Sixteen Football League Clubs host women's Cup football with Derby County, the 25th League club to stage a women's match.

1991 – England goalkeeper Therese Wiseman equals the record of caps held by former England forward, Linda Curl. She won her 60th cap playing in a friendly against Scotland on April 20th at Wycombe Wanderers F.C.

The First ever Women's World Cup Finals to be held in China in November. The National Premier League is formed.

PLAY FOOTBALL...
THE GAZZA WAY

Corners and penalties

(Part Two)

Taken from the book SOCCER SKILLS WITH GAZZA by Paul Gascoigne and Mel Stein, published by Stanley Paul. Price: £6.99.

Two ways to take a penalty ... the instep power drive (left) and the placed side foot shot.

What sort of corners are there? Well, there's the long one beyond the far post; the corner to the far post; the near post; the short corner, the floater, the one that's whipped in, inswinger or outswinger ... the list is endless.

I'm a great believer in deciding drawn matches by the number of corners won. It shows which team has been attacking most.

If your forward line is six inches shorter than the opposition defence then the short corner, or the low hard corner will be more effective.

It is all about weighing up your best options, as with so many aspects of the game of football.

The corner I really fancy is the one I whip in as an inswinger, the weight and timing on the ball has to be perfect. Again it's all about practice.

Another thing to practice are penalties, even if you're not the regular penalty taker. You could be called upon in a shoot-out.

Keep your eye on the ball and your head down, avoiding any eye contact with the keeper. You've really got two choices with a penalty; blasting it or placing it. The important thing is to make up your mind beforehand where you're going to put it ... and never change your mind.

Shooting

'Shoot on sight' is not necessarily good advice. To have a shot at goal you must have a chance of scoring, otherwise hold the ball up or pass to someone in a better position.

Whether you're hitting the ball on the deck, or volleying it the important thing is to get your body right over the ball so it keeps low. Lean back and the ball flies high.

With the volley it's vital to keep your eye on the ball at all times. Don't look where you're intending to go and don't lift your head.

After you've hit the ball with full power you should end up with both feet off the ground.

Practice the dead ball shot but remember that the ball is moving more often than it's not so you have to get used to that. Shooting is all about accuracy so practice with small goals or by chalking numbers on a wall.

The half-volley is another useful technique to master. It's all about accuracy and timing. It is also an exception to the general rule of shooting. Don't lean over the ball, lean back but keep your toes pointed down.

Knee over the ball to keep the shot down. Right: Full instep volley impact.

A power drive from a stationary ball. Both feet off the ground ... the perfect balance.

Dribbling and running

In order to dribble with the ball, the one thing you need more than anything else is confidence. If you feel you can go forward with the ball and take people on, then do it. It's the most exciting thing to watch in a game.

There's an element of body swerve in a good dribbling run, an element of balance, there's ball control and maybe the drop of a shoulder and the dummy.

But what you also need to be able to do is change your pace. It's not just about running at speed, what I think is more effective is ringing the changes in pace – as if you have got different gears.

NOBBY

OUR GOALIE GOT STRANDED IN THE SNOW

SO WE PUT A SNOWMAN IN HIS PLACE

AND WHAT A STAR — PURE MAGIC!

HE WAS A DEAD CERT FOR 'MAN OF THE MATCH' UNTIL HE FADED IN THE SECOND HALF

FADED! HOW CAN A SNOWMAN POSSIBLY FADE?

THE SUN CAME OUT AND HE MELTED!

The White switch for City

David White is destined for a big future. He masterminded Manchester City's impressive flourish during the final weeks of last season when he emerged as a goalscoring striker.

On his own admission it's a role that came about by chance when player-manager, Peter Reid, made several positional changes to accommodate the return of Neil Pointon to the side.

As a result, the City boss decided to switch White into the middle to form a new partnership with Niall Quinn. To the surprise of everyone concerned the move worked like a dream as the two players immediately struck up a fine understanding.

The result was that White suddenly began hitting home the goals with the highlight being his four goal performance in the run-away win against Aston Villa at Villa Park.

White, who played for England B last season, admitted: "I'm not really sure even now how the switch came about.

"But what I do know is that I've had the most successful season of my career and just as important the team played really well.

"Everything suddenly became easy. The players began operating together as a team and I think that it could be the start of something big for Manchester City if this kind of progress can be maintained."

White has obviously set his heart on playing for England and if he can maintain the form he displayed in the closing weeks of last season he could be one of the players emerging for the next World Cup.

He said: "Graham Taylor has said that he will always go for the player in form.

"I'm just hoping that I can keep scoring and then I might stand a chance of a full cap."

White has paid credit to Quinn for his improved goalscoring form.

"He creates the space and makes everything happen," says White. "It is certainly a new experience to be playing in the heart of the attack and scoring so many goals is a tremendous boost to my career."

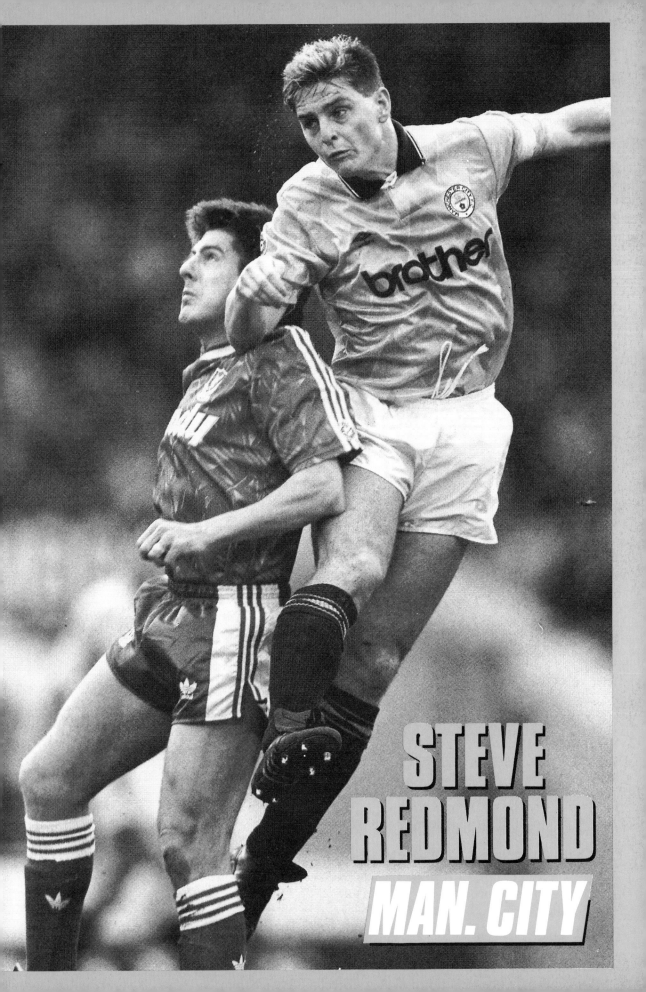

STEVE
REDMOND

MAN. CITY

Maracana

**Brazil 0,
England 2
1984 tour**

Azteca

**Argentina 3,
West Germany 2
1986 World Cup Final**

GREAT G

San Siro

**Shared by
AC Milan and Inter**

Bernabeu

**The home of Real Madrid
(white) in action v Real Sociedad**

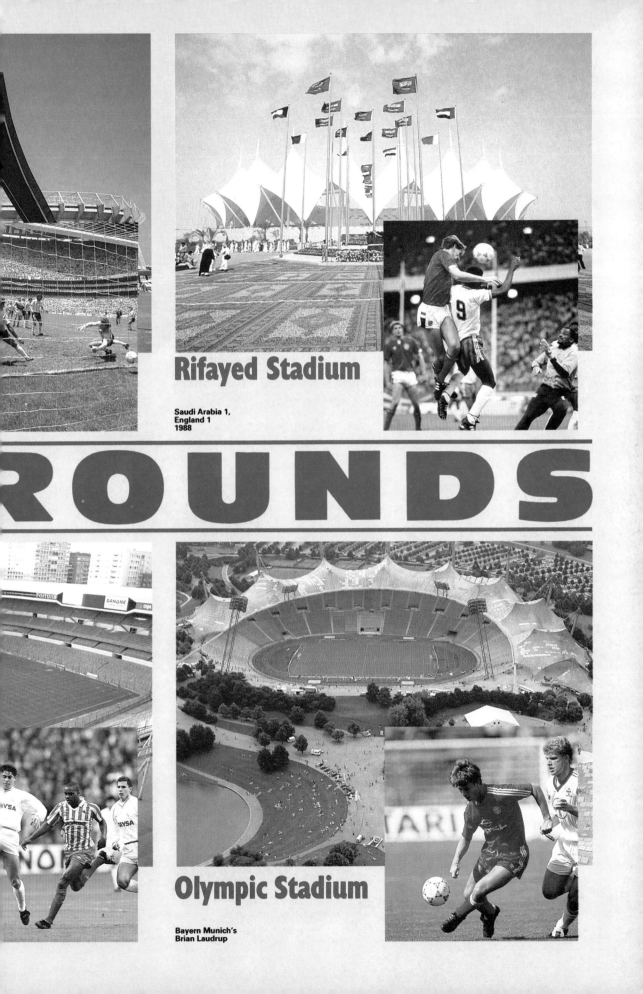

Rifayed Stadium

**Saudi Arabia 1,
England 1
1988**

ROUNDS

Olympic Stadium

**Bayern Munich's
Brian Laudrup**

Gordon Bradley saves the day for Leicester in the 1949 FA Cup Final against Wolves

Bruce Grobbelaar scored a penalty on his last game for Crewe

HERE'S a quick quiz question for you: name the odd one out among Peter Shilton, Ray Clemence and Pat Jennings.

The answer is Clemence, the only one of the three great goalkeepers who never SCORED a goal in a first-class match.

Not surprisingly, really, for very few goalkeepers do get on the scoring list. But there have been a few who did, through freak kicks from hand, going into an outfield position after injury, or even taking penalties.

Jennings and Shilton both scored one goal apiece in the course of lengthy careers, curiously enough in the same year.

Jennings, playing for Spurs, began the l967-68 season by scoring with a huge kick in the Charity Shield match against Manchester United at Old Trafford, and in the following

October Shilton repeated that feat when playing for Leicester against Southampton, one of the clubs he later joined.

The goalkeeper Shilton beat – one of the few goals by a No. 1 captured by television – bounced in over Alex Stepney. And in due course he went on to achieve a particularly novel distinction for a 'keeper.

At Christmas 1973 Manchester United had scored only 18 goals in 21 First Division matches, and Stepney was joint top scorer with two, both from penalties.

For a time it seemed as if he would overhaul the League record of five goals in one season by a 'keeper, Chesterfield's Arnold Birch, with five penalties in 1923-24.

The first of Stepney's penalties was against Leicester. And who was the City goalkeeper? Shilton, of course.

Not that Leicester weren't used to 'keepers scoring against them. In the 1950s Fulham and Scotland 'keeper Ian Black headed a goal against them after injuring a hand and moving into attack – no substitutes in those days – and a few years later Notts County's Gordon Bradley did the same. That was really cruel, for Bradley was a former Leicester player and had kept goal for them in the 1949 F.A. Cup Final.

Two 'keepers scored on the same day in 1963, in the first round of the Cup – Granger of York, against Halifax, and Terry Adlington of Torquay, against Barnet.

Exeter's Bernard Singleton gave himself a present on Christmas Day 1950 by moving out after injury and shooting a goal, and Reading's Arthur Wilkie deserves special mention by scoring twice against Halifax in l962. This is believed to be the only such instance in English

SCORING KEEPERS

Mighty Pat Jennings stunned the Old Trafford fans when he scored against United

soccer history.

There might even have been a case of a Wembley goal by a goalkeeper. Manchester United's Ray Wood broke his jaw early in the 1956 F.A. Cup Final against Aston Villa but returned later and played for half an hour on the right wing, semi-conscious and with blurred vision.

What a story that would have been if the gallant Wood had got a goal. He didn't, and Aston Villa went on to win 2-1. At least two goalkeepers have been chosen to play in outfield positions as a matter of policy, not in emergencies. John King of Swansea, capped once by Wales in his proper position, had a few games in his club's attack, and during the 1960s Tony Read of Luton added 28 games – and 12 goals – as a forward to his 195 appearances in goal.

We have been unable to trace any instance of a goalkeeper scoring in England from open play, other than when changing places with a colleague after injury – although we believe it has happened in South America.

But if we had to name the 'keeper most likely to manage it, we would go for Liverpool extrovert Bruce Grobbelaar.

Arthur Wilkie

He scored from a penalty in his last game for Crewe before going to Canada and then on to Liverpool and he is often seen roaming near the halfway line.

Perhaps one day, when Liverpool have a game well won, Brucie might go charging into the opposing half, and blast a shot past the rival 'keeper.

Imagine the uproar that would follow if he did that in front of the Kop!

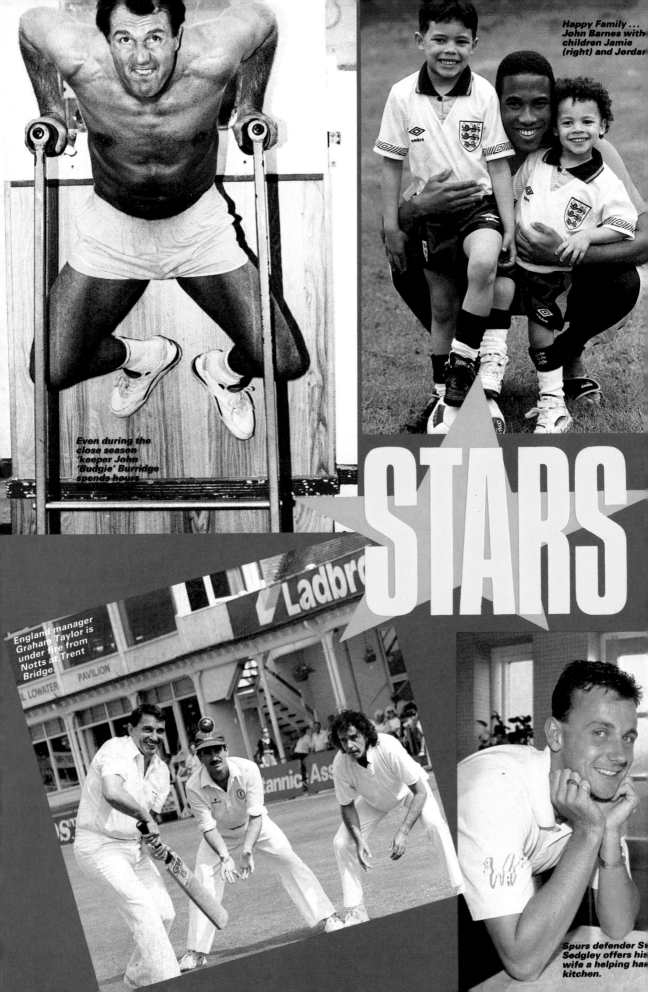

Even during the close season 'keeper John 'Budgie' Burridge spends hours

Happy Family ... John Barnes with children Jamie (right) and Jordan

STARS

England manager Graham Taylor is under fire from Notts at Trent Bridge.

Spurs defender Steve Sedgley offers his wife a helping hand kitchen.

est and England
ender Stuart
rce gets to
s with Twiggy,
hestnut hunter
t belongs to his
friend Liz

Sheffield United
hardman Vinny
Jones relaxes on
the Yorkshire
moors.

FF DUTY

Crystal Palace hot shots Ian Wright
and Mark Bright admire this vintage
hot-rod.

SPOTLIGHT ON

MIRACLE-WORKER

ALEX TOTTEN has worked a minor miracle in his time as manager of St. Johnstone.

He took charge in April, 1987, and admits: "The difference between then and now is like night and day. It has been a dramatic period for the club.

Totten turns back the clock to remember: "We were in the Second Division when I took over for the last game of the season. I had no time to assess the playing staff.

"We drew 1-1 with Raith Rovers and I arranged a few friendlies to have a look at the players. I ended up giving free transfers to 11 of them and we made a completely fresh start."

Totten celebrated his first season in charge by leading Saints to promotion and the following year they took Rangers to a replay in the Semi-Final of the Scottish Cup.

Saints kept the momentum going to win the First Division in 1990 and, to most people's amazement, took the step-up to the top flight in their stride.

THANKS, SHANKS

THE late, great Bill Shankly had a profound effect on Saints boss Alex Totten.

It was at Anfield that the young Totten, straight from school, launched his football career. But he failed to make the grade with the mighty Liverpool.

However, he still learned a lot. "It was a real education," he says. "I like to think a lot of Shanks has rubbed off on me.

"The thing I remember most was the way he treated people. I was just an apprentice but he made me feel just as important as Roger Hunt, Ron

Yeats and the other first team stars.

"He was so thorough, so professional, and the good habits I learned at Anfield have stuck with me ever since."

McGINNIS STEPS UP

SKIPPER Gary McGinnis is adamant that Saints belong in the big-time.

He was transferred from Dundee United in February, 1990, and some people might have seen it as a step back. But he has no regrets.

"At the time, Saints were in the First Division," he recalls. "But I still saw it as a forward move and I think I've been proved correct."

The former Scotland Under-21 cap adds: "What we've achieved so far is just the beginning. We can get better still and establish the club as one of the very best."

Andy Brehme – the answer to 22

Paul Ince – 15 Across

ANSWERS

1. Midfield. 2. Czechoslovakia. 3. Belgium. 4. Marseille. 5. Montpellier. 6. Real. 7. Gullit and Van Basten. 8. One. 9. Morten Olsen. 10. Toto. 11. The longest time without conceding a goal in international football. 12. Sweden. 13. Bayern Munich. 14. Sweden. 15. Real Madrid. 16. Tottenham. 17. Robert Prosinecki. 18. Goycochea. 19. 1985 clash between Manchester United and Everton. 20. He was out for the season through injury. 21. 1984. 22. Andy Brehme. 23. Overhead kick. 24. Brazil. 25. Two.

Crossword (page 64) Across: 1. Broomfield. 8. Jags. 9. Red Devil. 10. Tigers. 11. Andrew (s). 12. Ten. 13. Gary. 15. Ince. 17. Pro. 19. Gretna. 21. Newell. 23. Arie Haan. 24. Book. 25. The Clarets.
Down: 2. Reading. 3. Ossie. 4. Forest. 5. Endean. 6. Dresden. 7. Price. 14. Retreat. 16. Elliott. 17. Palace. 18. One-nil. 20 Re- run. 22. Weber.

ST. JOHNSTONE

SERGEI MARK II

SAINTS fans have got it wrong when they chant: "There's only one Sergei Baltacha".

The experienced Soviet Union international has a son, 12-year-old Sergei Junior, who is being tipped as a star of the future.

The youngster established a scoring reputation with Suffolk boys' team Whitton Sports after Dad arrived in Britain to join Ipswich Town.

Then, when his father was transferred North of the border, young Sergei hit the goal trail again for Perth team Oakbank.

His exploits caught the attention of a Tottenham scout and the lad eagerly accepted an invitation for trials at White Hart Lane.

But St. Johnstone are also hoping to snap up Baltacha Mark II. Manager Alex Totten says: "The boy is way ahead of his time.

"He's an absolute natural and I don't even want to think about the possibility of him going elsewhere."

MINI IBROX

SAINTS' switch to their plush, new McDiarmid Park headquarters in 1989 underlined the club's ambition to rub shoulders with Scottish football's top brass.

The move was voted a huge hit by players and supporters alike. Star striker Roddy Grant says: "It's brilliant – streets ahead of most Scottish grounds.

"Maybe it only holds 10,000 but the atmosphere when it is full is absolutely electric. All the lads get a terrific buzz from it."

The all-seater stadium, complete with adjacent artificial training pitch, has been dubbed mini-Ibrox because it was modelled on Rangers' showpiece ground.

TREVOR FRANCIS:
A man in a million

From the moment he stepped on to the soccer stage as a 16-year-old kid they labelled 'Superboy', it was blatantly obvious Trevor Francis was going to be a star.

But, who'd have thought that, after more than 20 years at the top and now fewer than THREE million pound moves, he would still be turning on the style?

Trevor reckons he can go on playing at the top level until he's 40 and few who saw him in action for Sheffield Wednesday last season would argue with that.

As Wednesday clinched promotion back to Division One last season, Francis seemed to roll back the years with the ease with which he has been tormenting defenders since he burst on to the scene with Birmingham as a teenager.

He made his debut as a substitute against Cardiff at the start of the 1970-71 season, before playing his first full game against Oxford the following week. At 16 he was public property, but thrived on the adulation he received.

Fifteen goals in his first 15 games made him an instant hit with the St. Andrews faithful as he struck up an immediate understanding with Bob Latchford.

By the end of only his second season he had helped City clinch promotion to the First Division. He was only 18 but, already, a sought-after figure.

As Trevor's career progressed and his rare talent developed, Everton, Manchester United and Derby were among the clubs chasing him.

It took him almost four years to realise his ambition of playing for a 'big' club, however, and it was Brian Clough who smashed the British transfer record by signing him for Nottingham Forest in the first ever million pound deal.

So, in February 1979, he set about the task of helping Forest retain the League title and lift the European Cup.

Having kicked off his new career in humble circumstances, in front of 20 people in the Forest A team, he was soon the goalscoring hero of the

Goalscoring hero for Birmingham at just 16.

club's European Cup triumph over Malmo.

He missed the victory over Hamburg in the same competition a year later because of injury and, by the summer of 1981, he was on the move again.

It was another million pound deal which took him to Manchester City.

His stay at Maine Road was short but sweet and, after just one season, the financial screw had tightened so much that City decided to offload Francis, by then an established England international, to Sampdoria in Italy. The fee? Yet another cool million.

Injuries

Trevor had already experienced a couple of spells overseas in the North American Soccer League, but this was the real thing.

Injuries, however, were to plague him throughout his five-year stint in Italy, first with Sampdoria and finally with Atalanta.

Together with Graeme Souness he helped Sampdoria win the Italian Cup in 1985, but honours were few and far between.

By the end of the 1985-86 season, following the emergence of rising star Luca Vialli, he had to make the sad decision to leave. Again he looked like joining Manchester United but chose to stay in Italy with Atalanta.

A year later though he was finally on his way home. Not to Old Trafford, but to Ibrox.

In his nine months as a Rangers player, however, Francis made just 19 appearances – most as sub – and, apart from a penalty in a Skol Cup shoot-out, he failed to score.

From Glasgow Rangers he went to Queens Park Rangers, a move which eventually took him into the realms of soccer management – and out again almost as quickly.

He was named player-boss in December 1988 but after just 11 months, during which time he was involved in 19 transfer dealings, he was sacked.

For the first time in his career he came in for merciless criticism – although it wasn't his only disappointment in a glittering career.

One of the biggest blows he had to contend with was being axed from the England squad for the 1986 World Cup finals. His England career ended at the age of 32 when he felt he still had a lot to offer his country.

Since leaving QPR and finally teaming up with Ron Atkinson at the third time of asking, Trevor continued to weave his magic with Sheffield Wednesday.

A key member of the squad which won the Rumbelows Cup and celebrated an instant return to top flight football after just one season in the Second Division, he is still going strong.

European Cup winner for Forest against Malmo.

Debut for Man. City against Stoke.

Striking for England against the Czechs in the 1982 World Cup finals.

A life of luxury with Sampdoria team-mate Graeme Souness.

Double success with Ron Atkinson at Sheffield Wednesday.

Welcome To **HILLSBOROU**

TERRY-FIC FACTS ABOUT TV

We put the spotlight on Terry Venables, one of the game's most colourful characters ...

Full name: Terence Frederick Venables
Date of birth: 6th January,1943 in Dagenham, Essex
Family: Terry's marriage to Christine ended in divorce six years ago. They have two daughters, Nancy 24 and Tracy, 22. He is a proud grandad to Nancy's three-year-old son, Sam.
School: He attended Lymington Secondary School in Dagenham and left at 15 without any qualifications.
Professional career: A thinking midfielder he turned professional with Chelsea in August 1960, after failing to make the Great Britain Olympic soccer squad. Played 202 League games and scored 26 goals before moving to Tottenham Hotspur in May 1966. Scored five goals in 114

League appearances for Spurs and was then transferred to QPR in June 1969. Played 178 League games and scored 19 goals before moving across London to Crystal Palace in September 1974. He ended his playing career 14 League matches later to become manager of the club. Built what was described at the Team of the Eighties and then left to take over as boss at QPR. Led Rangers to an FA Cup Final appearance against Tottenham in 1982. Resigned a couple of years later to become manager of Barcelona.Took them to the Spanish Championship before leaving in December 1987 to succeed David Pleat as Spurs boss in December 1987. Despite the financial traumas of last season, Terry took Spurs to FA

Terry took a typing course to help his business and writing exploits

With close friend and rival George Graham

Cup Final victory and a respectable position in the First Division.
International honours: Would have played for Wales if his late Welsh mother Myrtle had had her way. Instead won England caps at EVERY level – amateur, schoolboy, youth, Under-23, B and full international. Despite that impressive record he only played twice in the senior side, against Holland and Belgium in 1965.
Schoolboy heroes: Former Tottenham and Northern Ireland captain Danny Blanchflower and the late Duncan Edwards of Manchester United and England, who was killed in the Munich Air Disaster.
Friends in the game: He is close to Arsenal manager George Graham. Terry was George's best man at his wedding and gave him his first coaching job at Crystal Palace.
Outside interests: A successful business man off the park, Terry owns pubs, a bar in London's West End, an exclusive dining club in fashionable Kensington and property in Spain and England. He invented a board game called The Manager which has become a top seller. Also an accomplished author and co-wrote a TV detective series called 'Hazell' and a football novel called 'They Used To Play On Grass'. A good singer, Terry once performed with the Joe Loss Band at the Hammersmith Palais.
Favourite singers and actors: Frank Sinatra, Nat King Cole and Walter Matthau who starred in his favourite all-time film 'The Odd Couple'.
Favourite meal and drink: Steak and kidney pudding, sausages, lager and champagne.
Favourite thing: A gold ring given to him by his mother.

Pep talk for his QPR players before extra-time against Spurs in the 1982 FA Cup Final. The game ended 1-1 and Spurs won the replay 1-0.

Terry joined Spurs in May, 1966

Near miss . . . Mo Johnston goes close for Rangers in another Old Firm clash against Celtic.